SIX STEPS TO
ENTREPRENEURIAL
SUCCESS

THE START-UP
J CURVE

HOWARD LOVE

GREENLEAF
BOOK GROUP PRESS

Published by Greenleaf Book Group Press
Austin, Texas
www.gbgpress.com

Distributed by Greenleaf Book Group

For ordering information or special discounts for bulk purchases, please contact Greenleaf Book Group at PO Box 91869, Austin, TX 78709, 512.891.6100.

Design and composition by Greenleaf Book Group
Cover design by Greenleaf Book Group

Cataloging-in-Publication data is available.

Print ISBN: 978-1-62634-292-7

eBook ISBN: 978-1-62634-293-4

Part of the Tree Neutral® program, which offsets the number of trees consumed in the production and printing of this book by taking proactive steps, such as planting trees in direct proportion to the number of trees used: www.treeneutral.com

TreeNeutral®

Printed in the United States of America on acid-free paper
16 17 18 19 20 21 22 23 24 25   10 9 8 7 6 5 4 3 2 1
First Edition

CONTENTS

INTRODUCTION

Although there are some good books on start-ups out there, this is the one I wish I had read before I began my first start-up thirty-five years ago. Each of the fifteen start-ups I have either founded or cofounded would have benefited from the knowledge contained in these pages. And no doubt, the over fifty investments I have made in various start-ups, as an angel investor, would also have benefited if I knew then what I know now.

When I first considered writing this book, I made sure nobody had published anything like it. As an angel investor, I've found that when I have a new idea, or I'm presented with one by a member of my team, it seems like we're the first to have thought of it. With a little research, however, I often find that someone has already beaten us to market. For this reason, I checked out the start-up/entrepreneurial body of literature, and while I did find a number of useful books, I did not find anything like this one. The books that were available tended to offer specific point solutions to common specific start-up challenges or case histories, rather than guide start-up founders on their entire start-up journey. You can find some books that focus on certain aspects of the journey but nothing that gives you the complete tour.

As this book's first chapter explains, a start-up unfolds in a predictable pattern; the more aware you are of this pattern, the better able you will be to capitalize on it. Instead of feeling lost and confused when you suffer a setback—something that happens to start-ups quite frequently in their initial stages—you'll be able to put these problems in context. This is not only psychologically reassuring but also helps you know what to do—and what not to do—at a particular moment in time. By knowing exactly where you are on the path, and what to do at that point in time, your odds of success will increase, and you will get to success faster.

Each chapter includes examples and stories that illustrate a start-up's evolution, many taken from my own experiences, and some from those of other well-known start-up founders. You'll also find a lot of advice to help you take the right action at the right time and avoid the common traps along the way—I'll end each chapter with an assessment tool that will help you personalize this advice. I've shown early drafts of this book to entrepreneur friends, and their common refrain is, "Yeah, I sure wish I would have had this book years ago, before I started my first company!"

I'm also writing this book to let you know that you are not alone; your difficult experiences are similar to what many start-up founders experience. You are on a path that is well trodden, but if you don't know what others have gone through, you will probably feel all alone in the wilderness. Many of the toughest issues are difficult to discuss with your employees and your board for a wide variety of reasons. It is my hope that this book will have a positive effect on your angst, reassuring you that other entrepreneurs have faced the same difficult issues.

The advice I'm offering you came to me the hard way—through many successes and failures over the last thirty-five years. The failures have been a critical part of my education, and history has taught me that the price of education goes up substantially after college. Though I've been fortunate that the successes have trumped the failures, I am sure my postgraduate education has cost me many millions of dollars. While I wouldn't want to change my journey, there is little doubt in my mind that if I had read this book early in my career, I would have saved myself a lot of time, money, and heartache. Through this book, I'd like to give you the benefit of my rather expensive education and get you to start-up success as swiftly as possible. Let me give you a brief description of those thirty-five years and how they shaped the perspective presented in this book.

My first tech start-up was at Colgate University, where I was (sort of) attending college. I say *sort of* because, while I certainly worked far harder than the average student, I was working at making money, not grades. My partner was a friend and fellow Colgate student, Cliff Ribaudo. We were a classic entrepreneurial team: Cliff was the tech guy who did all the coding, and I did "everything else," whatever that happened to be. That company (eventually called Inmark Development) started out doing research on trading systems for the stock and futures markets, but we didn't have a financially viable model, so we needed to try another angle. It only made sense to make use of our skills and assets. Around this time the first IBM PC was introduced, and we bought one and decided to make a packaged software product for individual investors that we could sell. That was to be my first experience at what I call a *morph,* which is a fundamental shift in the business product or strategy. Our first packaged software product, called Market Maker, did OK but still was not enough to create a sustainable company, so we morphed again and got original equipment manufacturer (OEM) licensing deals with many of the large quote vendors that sold real-time information to Wall Street.

That sustained us for a while, but it became obvious that this was going to leave us well short of our aspirations. We were fortunate to have some brilliant engineers, including fellow cofounder Mark Anders; Peter Handsman, chief technology officer (CTO); and others who had come up with an ingenious way to write code once and then deploy it on multiple operating systems, such as Windows, Mac, Unix, and OS/2. It was a big idea and quite a technical feat. So we made one final morph into the development tools market, where we developed what was technically referred to as a "cross platform, object-oriented application framework," and we called it zApp. In order to find more engineers, we moved to Mountain View, California, and went all-in. Eventually, that product did well, and we ended up going public after we merged with another company. We had started out at Colgate, in upstate New York, developing financial market trading systems, and ended up in Silicon Valley selling software development tools—that was a journey indeed.

Looking back at this initial business, as well as many others I had helped start or invested in—usually with my venture partner, David Hehman—we noted how many of the companies we had invested in had gone through near-death experiences and morphed into companies and products that didn't look anything like what was in the original business plan. In fact, it was rare for a company to stick with the business plan and execute it as it was first conceived. Further, we realized that if you dug into the individual history of many well-known start-ups, as well as those in our own portfolio, this pattern was common indeed. Pinterest began as Tote, which was an e-commerce enabling app where users could track their favorite retailers. William Wrigley used a free piece of chewing gum to help sell his primary products of soap and baking powder, until he realized that the chewing gum was more popular. The photo-sharing tool Flickr started out as a role-playing game called Game Neverending. Groupon was originally a socially responsible fund-raising site called The Point. Twitter began as Odeo, a podcast service that they realized was doomed when Apple debuted iTunes. The list is endless.

This was my "aha!" moment—the epiphany that drove me to write this book. Most entrepreneurs believe that their original business plan will work; much of the start-up literature appears to share this belief. As veteran investors, however, David and I had learned that the original plan almost never works. In fact, it's my belief, backed up by many conversations with start-up veterans, that drastic (not incremental) revisions to the original business plan happen in over 80 percent of successful start-ups. It struck us that if entrepreneurs entered their start-ups with realistic expectations—if they recognized that they would have to revise their original plan at least once (and probably twice or three times) and if they knew what to do along the road—then they would vastly increase their chances for success.

As David and I talked, we realized that many start-ups fail because founders and investors harbor all sorts of misconceptions about the path before them. If they possessed a clear vision of the real road ahead, a map that would show them where they were and what to focus on at that point in the journey, they would be able to move forward with greater speed, assurance, and effectiveness. This road consists of six predictable steps or phases: Create, Release, Morph, Model, Scale, and Harvest. Each of these phases requires a primary focus and poses specific challenges. Knowing these phases and how to traverse them the right way is crucial.

Further, I realized that these six phases make up a graphic form, a curve that represents the value of the enterprise at any given point along the path. I dubbed that form the *Start-Up J Curve*, and its shape suggests how the value of the enterprise tends to decline over the first few phases, and the primary value creation develops in the latter stages. This J Curve form has far-reaching implications that we will explore throughout the book.

Every year, David and I host a start-up CEO conference where we invite the leaders of our most promising companies to gather to work as a group and help one another out by offering solutions to their largest challenges. During one of these gatherings, I presented the theory of the J Curve and its six phases to our audience. During one of these presentations, I noticed some of the CEOs were taking pictures of the slides; this and other responses demonstrated that the six-phase model was resonating with them. That's when I realized the value of this start-up roadmap and the need to communicate it to a wider audience. I started showing it to some of my venture capital friends in Silicon Valley, and they also found the model predictive and useful. As one good friend remarked, "It has the virtue of being correct!"

As you read, you'll find a number of concepts that may seem counterintuitive or at least contrary to conventional wisdom, including my suggestions that you embrace the unknown and make failure your friend, that it is best to have too little money rather than too much, and that your naïveté is a virtue. All I ask is that you examine these ideas with an open mind as I demonstrate why I believe they are valid and valuable and can help you substantially increase your odds of success.

Finally, let me leave you with two additional pieces of advice before I introduce the J Curve. First, recognize that the model I'm going to present provides general rules, and there are always exceptions to these rules. For instance, in the Scale chapter, I'm going to assert that you should never scale before you nail the business model.

If you know your start-up history, however, you may recall that Facebook and Twitter scaled before they had nailed their model. Perhaps you'll be the next Facebook or Twitter. More likely, however, your start-up will follow the J Curve path, and you'll be successful because you waited until the right moment to scale.

Second, in the process of pointing out potential traps and pitfalls, I'm going to talk about how difficult start-ups can be. There is no way around that—start-ups are *hard*, and I'll point out many reasons. But I do this not to dissuade you from pursuing your start-up dream but rather to prepare you so that you will be in a better position to meet the inevitable substantial challenges as they arise. Despite the seeming pessimism that comes with these warnings, I'm optimistic that start-up founders can surmount the problems they encounter through the use of the J Curve. Knowing about these challenges and potential setbacks will help you prepare for them and get past them.

Because of my personal background, the perspective I offer in this book is usually Internet or software related, but I would suggest that the primary principles would remain intact for almost any start-up. Of course, I would expect that there are adjustments, depending on the industry you are in, but I believe the J Curve is a metaphor that will be highly useful for any start-up effort.

As a start-up founder, you're doing something that's not only exciting and potentially highly profitable, but you're also doing something necessary. In order to move forward, the world needs start-ups, the world needs innovation, and the world needs people like you to strike out on an adventure. It's rare that large companies or governments create groundbreaking innovations (though I do show later in the book how they can do this much better). Breakthroughs in all fields usually occur because of hungry, enterprising individuals and small groups of individuals that band together to bring a crazy, seemingly foolish idea into reality. There are over 2.5 million new businesses started in the US each year. If you have a crazy idea that you are passionate about, first read this book, and if you are still fired up, I suggest considering Richard Branson's slogan: "Screw it, let's do it!"

1

THE VALUE OF A MAP

Start-ups are hot. We're seeing not only more entrepreneurial businesses emerge in the twenty-first century but also a more diverse group of start-ups. Besides the college students, recent graduates, and serial entrepreneurs who have always occupied this space, a variety of other participants are becoming more numerous: corporate executives fleeing the world of big business to create something on their own; brilliant young people whose first or second jobs may be with start-ups; refugees from nonprofit, government, and other sectors who are attracted to the entrepreneurial adventure. Additionally, start-up fever is spreading geographically throughout the US and also the world. It's not limited to Silicon Valley, Austin, and Seattle. Now start-ups, incubators, and accelerators are popping up in Pittsburgh, Chicago, Barcelona, and Shanghai. Tel Aviv, San Paulo, Sydney, and Bangalore now rank among the world's top twenty start-up ecosystems, according to the Startup Genome Project.

In addition, entrepreneurs are launching these new businesses at a time of great volatility and unpredictability. In our increasingly global, digital universe, nothing stays the same for long. Trends come and go with lightning speed, new, dominant companies emerge seemingly out of nowhere, and what's state-of-the-art today becomes hopelessly outmoded tomorrow.

Start-ups are hard. Very, very hard. They will likely test your creativity, perseverance, courage, and intelligence. Your relationships will also be tested—both within your company and with your family and friends. More than once, you are likely to be spent physically, emotionally, mentally, and financially.

This book will provide you with guidance, in bad times as well as good. It will give you a clear road map that will help you navigate the treacherous start-up terrain and make the journey to success as smooth and efficient as possible. This book will help you know with some level of certainty exactly where you are and what you need to be focusing on. I'll also try to expose the many myths that are associated with start-ups, and I'll try to point out the areas where you may need to alter your ingrained beliefs and patterns of thinking to increase the odds of both you and your start-up being successful.

More so than ever before, start-ups require a map to chart a course through innumerable and significant obstacles. As you'll discover, a map is exactly what this book will provide.

KNOW WHERE YOU'VE BEEN, WHERE YOU ARE, WHERE YOU'RE GOING

Start-ups aren't as random and chaotic as they might appear. If I've learned nothing else after thirty-five years of doing start-ups, it's that they begin, progress, and end in predictable ways. On a granular level, of course, the unexpected often happens; a funding source suddenly dries up, and a new customer appears seemingly out of nowhere. If you take the long view, however, you can see patterns to start-ups—patterns that can prove invaluable to entrepreneurs, providing perspective and assisting in decision making.

These patterns provide a map that entrepreneurs can follow, and this map can make the difference between failure and success, between making a small and large profit, and between having a flash-in-the-pan business and a sustainable one.

The value of this book is that it will help you become familiar with the start-up path. It will show you the markers along the way that will identify your particular point in the process and the best actions to take at this point. You'll learn, for instance, what to do when your initial product falters—a common start-up occurrence. You will also learn when to use the knowledge gleaned from the failing product to introduce iterative—and eventually, more successful—versions of the original.

Once you know where you are on the start-up path, you are much better able to know what your next steps should be—as well as the common (but avoidable) mistakes often made at a particular point on the path. This knowledge is hugely valuable tactically, but it's equally important psychologically. Too often, entrepreneurs give up prematurely when faced with surmountable obstacles, and they move forward aggressively when they should stop, reflect, and re-create.

Psychologically speaking, some entrepreneurs fold their businesses because it seems all is lost. When they are aware of the reality—they've just hit a speed bump—they can process the predicament, see it in context, and move forward rather than calling it quits. Similarly, some entrepreneurs take enormous and often unnecessary risks because they are caught up in the start-up mentality; they believe they must be overly aggressive if they're going to be successful. In fact, there are times to be aggressive and times to be conservative, and if they know where they are on the start-up map, they can respond appropriately.

Consider, too, that in the start-up universe, you always have more tasks to accomplish than time or resources to do them. The scarcity of resources is often extreme given the enormity of the mission, so efficiency becomes a critical discipline. Therefore, allocating the right amount of money and energy to the right tasks at the right moment is crucial. With a map in hand, this allocation is much easier to do than when you're flying by the seat of your pants and potentially flailing in too many directions.

As I noted in the introduction, I call this map the J Curve, and I'll help you become more familiar with its components shortly. First, though, I'd like to tell you about a start-up journey that helped open my eyes to the concept of the J Curve.

NO STRAIGHT LINE FROM START TO FINISH

In 2007, my business partner, David Hehman, and I helped Sara Sutton Fell launch a company that focused on connecting people who wanted to work from home with employers who supported remote workers. Since my own company, LoveToKnow, was a virtual organization, I knew from firsthand experience the value of working from home and that a huge untapped pool of talent preferred this option to an on-site office job. We were all incredibly excited. I knew Sara was the perfect one to lead the company because she is smart, effective, tenacious, and a hard worker—I'd witnessed these qualities when she did some marketing consulting for me at LoveToKnow. She also cofounded another start-up called JobsDirect, so she knew the jobs space. Sara was a multitool player who could cover wide swaths of responsibility. Perhaps more importantly, she is a wonderful human being who any savvy angel investor would trust. We teamed her up with an incredibly talented local engineer and another skilled engineer from India who helped with the original coding.

With great optimism, we released our first product, a curated selection of work-from-home jobs. Our proposed business model resembled that of other online companies featuring job sites; we charged prospective employers to post jobs and obtain access to our pool of job seekers.

Soon after the launch, however, we discovered that HR departments were tough prospective customers. They didn't have much money, and they were not inclined to try new things. Generally, they were also suspicious of and resistant to the work-at-home market. Despite our best efforts, we weren't having much success. While Sara maintained her optimism and persevered, the company was rapidly running out of money and not showing enough traction to justify investing more money. We plodded on for a few more months but were becoming more and more dejected, and then we discussed ending the venture.

Before doing so, though, we asked a simple question: Is there anything we are doing that is working? Sara pointed out that we had a huge number of job seekers who had created accounts and that they liked our site. As we reflected and discussed the situation, we recognized that we had proven at least one of our hypotheses: There was a huge untapped work-from-home labor market. They wanted and needed good jobs. Many competitive sites offering these remote jobs were often outright scams; in order to "work at home and make $xxx per day" you had to first buy the course or kit. No doubt, once these sites sold the kit, customers were disappointed with their subsequent "job" results.

Stay-at-home moms and others in our target market wanted real jobs, and we were one of the only sites that had them all in one place. So we decided to turn the model completely upside down, and instead of charging the prospective employers for job listings, we would charge the job seekers a monthly subscription. Because we made our service free to these employers, we began receiving great access to all of their remote jobs. Sara and her team quickly put up a test where we charged a nominal fee of fifteen dollars per month for job seekers to use our site. We obtained sign-ups immediately, and after a week, we became convinced that we could make real revenue. Today, FlexJobs is going gangbusters under Sara's adept leadership and the technical prowess of the incredibly talented CTO, Peter Handsman. And perhaps most importantly, we have helped over a million job seekers in their search for remote and flexible work.

We experienced a similar pattern with other companies in which we invested. Before FlexJobs, I had assumed that most successful companies developed their business plan and went with it until it passed or failed. What I came to realize, however, is that the entire journey is a process. The product and associated business model is really simply a hypothesis (not a hard-and-fast product launch), and the results are not pass/fail or black and white, but instead produce feedback, providing essential information that increases the odds of success. I had an epiphany: Iterations count more than the original idea, feedback counts more than the sales numbers, and flexibility and agility are more important than commitment to the original idea.

The straight line from start-up to sustainable success is largely a myth (though of course there are exceptions to this rule). Instead, start-ups usually follow a path that resembles the letter J.

THE SIX PHASES OF THE J CURVE

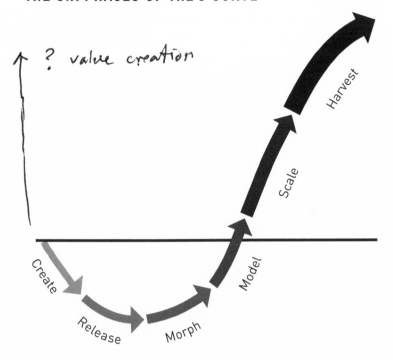

The shape of this six-phase curve suggests what differentiates it from other start-up models. As you can see, the base of the J represents the dip that occurs shortly after a company is launched. At first, the power of the business idea captures everyone's imagination, and it garners money, team members, and other forms of support. Then, reality sets in, products take longer to develop than expected, customers don't embrace the initial offering the way that was anticipated, the business model doesn't quite work, and eventually money starts drying up. These are all tough hits to take, especially if you're not prepared for them. Therefore, the dip is represented by the base of the J, and it's where start-ups figure it out or they die. I call it the *long, cold winter* or, if I'm feeling more morose, the *valley of death*.

Much of this book is dedicated to giving you strategies and tactics to get you and your start-up through that difficult period. Because once you are through it, you are into the steep upward slope of the J, and that is where the bulk of the value creation happens.

This curve is a reflection of start-up reality rather than an idealized progression. Each of the phases, listed in chronological order, reflect the challenges and opportunities that arise for all types of start-ups as they evolve. With this curve as your guide, you'll be able to put your start-up's experiences in context and have a better sense of what to do in response to these challenges and opportunities.

In chapters 2 through 7, I'll look at each phase in depth. For our purposes here, though, I'd like to provide you with a snapshot of each phase.

Phase 1—Create

This first phase of a start-up may seem self-evident, but numerous nuances exist that, if addressed, can get you off to a great rather than a fatally flawed start. In the Create phase, the three key elements are the idea, the team, and the money. Not all entrepreneurial ideas are created equal. Some are much better than others, and entrepreneurs need to recognize that the best ideas aren't manufactured, that superior technology does not automatically produce superior products, and that products succeed because they solve real problems or provide real new opportunities. So in this phase, start-ups must identify an idea that is going to be worthy of the entrepreneur investing their life's energy, not to mention their savings.

Similarly, they must raise money like the dickens; underestimating the amount of funds needed is a common failing. Contrary to what some entrepreneurs may believe, this is one of the best times to raise money from various sources. I like to characterize this initial phase as "dreams unburdened by reality." It can often be easier to raise funds while the excitement runs high and the story is virginal, as opposed to trying to do so when confronted by often-unforeseen challenges later in the process.

The team, too, can be a tricky proposition. Rugged individualism is a philosophy many entrepreneurs embrace, yet it can be counterproductive to start-up success. Putting together the strongest possible team with complementary skills and character traits is critical. Mistakes here will be hard to undo. Having a strong team of cofounders often serves start-ups better than solo entrepreneurs. Getting it right will make the endeavor both more successful and a lot more fun.

Phase 2—Release

Once the team, idea, and money are in place, it's time to get the initial product out there. In this phase, some entrepreneurs suffer from procrastination and/or perfectionism. These are the enemies. You have to push products into the market even when your impulse is to do more research, tinker with their formulation, or build more features.

After the product release, the most successful start-ups are the ones who listen the hardest. They pay close attention to what customers are telling them—both positive and negative feedback—and use it in the next phase. During release, entrepreneurs can't get too low or too high—they can't throw in the towel because of a negative response or expand frantically because of a positive one.

Phase 3—Morph

In most endeavors, people generally don't hit home runs their first time at bat. Generally, they don't get it right until they've had sufficient experiences—including failures—and learned from them. The same is true for start-ups, and that's why the Morph phase is so essential. In certain ways, it is the most important phase. This is where entrepreneurs take the feedback they've received after launching their initial product and make improvements, iterate, and/or pivot.

The goal here is to be flexible enough to move beyond the original idea and either make it better or use it as a stepping stone to something related but different. Admittedly, this can be difficult. Entrepreneurs tend to fall in love with their original ideas, and in this phase, they may need to alter or even largely abandon them. The keys to moving effectively through this phase are to listen and respond to customer feedback (it may be harsh, but it's true) and produce one or more fundamental changes, which I refer to as *morphs*, as fast as you can. By adapting in this manner, you increase the odds of finding a product that thrills your customers—and your investors.

Phase 4—Model

In this phase, you'll focus on nailing the business model. Your goal is to reach the point where if you put more investment money into the business, more cash will be generated. You need to get to the point where it's obvious that this company will generate cash flow at some certain point. You do this by knowing and driving down all your costs—customer acquisition, engineering, and so on—and at the same time maximizing your revenue. The Holy Grail is a large positive operating margin and concomitant large positive cash flow. You may decide to invest all of that positive cash flow into growth, and that's OK. But you should be honestly convinced the business model can and will generate cash. Otherwise you don't yet have a business.

Phase 5—Scale

The Scale phase is where much of the substantial value is typically created for investors. However, this can be a tricky stage for some entrepreneurs, in that they need to leave behind their small and insular mentality and build out the company. More specifically, this is the phase where you assemble the people, processes, and money necessary to take the company to the next level. You've morphed effectively. You've nailed the business model, and now it's time to tell the world about it, blow it out in the marketplace, and make something big. This is where your product and company can make its mark on the world, or as Steve Jobs liked to say, "put a dent in the universe." It also happens to be the best place to make real money.

Here, you must put in place the proper infrastructure to have a larger company; this requires new people, new processes, and usually, new money. The challenge may be that you like the people and processes that have gotten you this far, and you don't like the notion of major change—a requirement of the Scale phase. Another interesting challenge is receiving and accepting a lowball buyout offer. Having experienced tough times and facing the challenge of rapidly growing your business, you may be tempted to sell at the beginning of this critical juncture, just before adding significant value to the world and substantial wealth to your bank account.

Phase 6—Harvest

At this point in the life cycle, you are transitioning from start-up to a fully established business. As the name of this phase suggests, it's often time for entrepreneurs to reap what they've sown. This is a good thing, but it's also a complex one. At this point, the start-up is reaching maturity, and a lot of challenging decisions must be made: should you expand through acquisition or organically; should you take a great buyout offer; should you provide liquidity to investors through a buyback, IPO, or company sale?

This is a major transition point for the company, one where entrepreneurs need to think long and hard about short-term and long-term objectives. Major financial questions arise in this phase, and how to invest in the brand, as well as additional products, is a crucial one.

In addition, this may be the time for entrepreneurs to cash out or step aside, while for others, it's an opportunity for continued personal growth by diving into the challenge of taking the company into another sphere. To make these tough decisions, recognize how your entrepreneurial vision is coloring your decision making, and get past that biased perspective to determine what's best for the long-term interests of the company, including the investors, employees, customers, and you personally.

Harvest should be a fun time no matter what you decide. You've moved past the life-or-death choices and instead face "puffball" decisions—heads you win, tails you win more.

PUTTING THESE PHASES TO WORK

iSoccerPath is a start-up that offers high school athletes an education and evaluation service to guide families and players through the process of becoming a student athlete. The program is designed to facilitate Division I college acceptance and scholarships for elite high school soccer players. By offering everything from player portfolio assembly, training, and videos, iSoccerPath makes the brutally competitive and usually confusing process of becoming a college athlete easier to navigate. The market of parents seeking an edge for their soccer-playing children is sizable and receptive to the services offered by iSoccerPath.

Relatively early in the life of the start-up, iSoccerPath CEO Jeff Jaye came to see me to discuss global expansion, new products and services, and franchising possibilities. Like many entrepreneurs during the early phases of the J Curve, he was flying on adrenaline, kept aloft by his dream of what the business could become. Buoyed by the positive, initial reception iSoccerPath had received, Jeff was naturally excited.

But as I pointed out to him, he was putting the cart before the horse—or in start-up terms, his thinking was phase 5 (Scale) when he was in phase 3 (Morph). By showing Jeff the J Curve, I was able to help him recognize that he was in Morph but that his head was awash in scaling opportunities. Further, I suggested that the phase-appropriate activities were continuing to iterate his service, refine his product offering, obtain more customer traction, and then focus on the business and revenue model. Once he had accomplished these tasks successfully, he could move on and address the scaling opportunities that were already coming his way, if they still made sense.

I helped him understand that being out of phase is bad for the business. If he were to focus his attention on scaling opportunities at this point in time, he would not only neglect another crucial task such as creating new and better iterations, but he would also jump on opportunities before the company had matured sufficiently to take best advantage of them. Engaging in phase 5 and 6 activities when you are starting phase 3 is virtually certain to result in misery and likely to endanger the enterprise.

I also noted that being out of phase is bad for an entrepreneur's health. Running a start-up is an endurance test. It's highly stressful physically, financially, and emotionally. Therefore, entrepreneurs need to pace themselves. When they attempt to do the work of the wrong phases at the wrong time—or try and do multiple phase tasks simultaneously—they are doing too much. Burnout is a real danger, and the J Curve helps entrepreneurs guard against it. By working phase by phase, entrepreneurs keep their workload manageable and focused and thus are also able to manage their stress more effectively.

Jeff followed my advice (which is rare) and turned down all offers to partner or affiliate with all newcomers for at least twelve months. They successfully completed a beta of twelve families in all age groups, and soon after their official launch, got nineteen clubs with over twelve thousand soccer players to become part of the education program. iSoccerPath is now ramping up their sign-ups, and with the steady, more measured growth model, they are getting a lot of investor attention.

GETTING THE ORDER RIGHT (AFTER GETTING IT WRONG)

It's not unusual for entrepreneurs to get ahead of themselves. Like Jeff from iSoccerPath, they are aggressive and opportunistic, their pace accelerated by their hopes and dreams. Doing things in the wrong order, however, is one of the surest ways of sabotaging your start-up; and doing them in the right J Curve order is one of the best ways of ensuring its success.

Consider two of the most common chronology mistakes:

- Focusing on the business model before figuring out the product

- Scaling before nailing the product or business model

You're likely to make the first mistake because when you explain your new idea to people, you'll be peppered with questions such as, "How are you going to make money at that?" While you don't want to ignore that question completely, the real questions to ask yourself are "Can I make something people will really want?" and "Can I get customers to actually USE my product or service?" Because if you can't get people to use your product or service, then you are not going to make any money at it anyway. What history generally *has* proven is that if you can get customer traction, you can find a way to make money. By focusing too much on the revenue model, you may be creating a myopic view of what your idea should be and blocking yourself from considering some important paths for evolving your initial idea. However, it might be one of those alternate paths or a later iteration that brings you the most customer traction. In addition, you waste valuable time being overly focused on the business model early on because you don't yet know what the actual product will be. You may go through two, three, or more iterations of the product, and by the nth iteration, the model you created for the first iteration will be hopelessly inappropriate. Paradoxically, emphasizing a business model prematurely, you may block yourself from the best money-making opportunities. You've structured the company in a certain way and hired people with certain types of experience to capitalize on the first product. Most organizations aren't sufficiently agile to shift as their product shifts, so they may have the right product but the wrong business model.

It's only when you gain significant customer traction with a product iteration and you are through the Morph phase that you should you spend significant time on the business model. Avoiding this mistake requires patience, a virtue that some entrepreneurs find is in short supply. To develop this patience, take a lesson from Google.

In 1997, when they launched Google, founders Sergey Brin and Larry Page were still Stanford University students. The search engine market was quite crowded with myriad participants, but Brin and Page were convinced they could make a far better one that treated links coming into a site (or page) as indications of what the site was about and its quality. They devoted the vast majority of their time perfecting their search algorithm and were rewarded about a year later when *PC Magazine* named Google as the top search engine. Four months after winning this award, they made their first nontech hire—Omid Kordestani, who became their head of sales and focused on revenue and the business model. It wasn't until September 1999, almost two years after they launched the product, that Google rolled out AdWords, which became the company's primary revenue source and foundational to its business model. No doubt, Brin and Page knew they had something special two years before they focused on revenue, and they did have some rough idea that advertising was a likely source of that revenue. But they also thought that cobranded search, possibly through licensing their technology, was a revenue source. It must have been tempting to move ahead quickly and place large, ugly display ads before they perfected their product—that's what Yahoo and the other dominant search engines were doing at the time. Instead, Google demonstrated great patience, pursued the perfection of search, gained a huge loyal following, and only then focused on their business model and were rewarded in a way that start-up founders can only dream about. Consciously or not, they understood that if they nailed search, they could wait until the time was right to create and focus on the business model.

The second mistake—"scaling before nailing" the product and business model—can devastate a start-up financially. It's common for a company that is in the Release or Morph phase to decide that they need to implement an ambitious growth plan and the infrastructure that goes with it. In fact, they often think if they can simply scale up marketing, customer acceptance will come. While it's quite possible if they wait x number of months, they'll be ready for the Scale phase and can implement this plan effectively, implementing it prematurely before all the pieces are in place is highly perilous. Whatever flaws still exists in the product and the business model can prove fatal when scaling occurs prematurely. Scaling a flawed business model that's small turns it into a flawed business model that's big. Instead of bleeding a little money, you're now hemorrhaging major cash, and eventually, you'll slam into a wall.

In many instances, this mistake is made because a start-up has too much money early on. If you recall the late nineties tech boom, you'll remember how dot-coms scaled shortly after their inception because money was pouring into their coffers. Even if the dot-com bust hadn't happened, many of them would have gone under because they were scaling before they had nailed the business model, and in fact, a number of them had not even nailed the product. Unfortunately, an over-abundance of funds encourages sloppy behavior and can create the illusion that anything is possible, including ill-timed hyperexpansion.

To avoid this mistake, follow the sequence of the phases with nearly religious devotion. While valid exceptions to the sequencing may exist, they are atypical, so think long and hard before you try to skip a phase. Scale when it's time to scale and not before, no matter how much money you have or what the competition is doing. From a financial perspective, you want to preserve your cash during the Create, Release, Morph, and Model phases, since you're going to need it, no matter how well things go initially. For start-ups, negative financial surprises are par for the course, so you want to be fiscally conservative at least until you reach the Scale phase.

"WE DON'T NEED NO STINKIN' PLAN"

If you're like many entrepreneurs, you may not place much value on plans and models. The J Curve and its six phases may appear to be overly programmatic, restricting your ability to be spontaneous and instinctive. This is not the point of the J Curve, and it provides plenty of room for entrepreneurial creativity. In fact, the J Curve makes it easier to act boldly, quickly, and innovatively because it lets you know where your focus should be at a given moment in time. When you know what the key objectives are in the release phase, for instance, you're not distracted by myriad unrelated issues that might otherwise seem pressing and overwhelming. You can productively concentrate on a handful of key assignments rather than scores of them, giving yourself the opportunity to devote your full attention and creativity to them.

As important as business plans can be, the J Curve isn't that type of highly structured, nuts-and-bolts framework. Rather, I encourage you to look at your start-up as a journey. The J Curve is a map to get you from start to success in the most efficient, efficacious, and safe manner possible. With it you'll have higher odds of success, and you'll get there sooner. It offers you directions to get to your destination (ideally, great Google-like success), but you choose the route you take, set your speed, and determine the vehicle that will get you there.

Though you may be the most iconoclastic of entrepreneurs—you hate bureaucracy, meetings, strategies—you probably also hate what happens when you run into unexpected trouble. Suddenly, you find yourself short of money, dealing with customer complaints, or struggling with product acceptance. Nothing prepared you for this crisis point, and you need guidance.

The J Curve provides it. As the German Field Marshal, Helmuth von Moltke, once said, "No plan survives contact with the enemy," or, in this case, reality. Significant problems and challenges hit every start-up, and when that happens, the J Curve allows you to view and address the problems within a reality-based context. Whether your funding sources start drying up or you receive a lowball buyout offer, you will have the context of knowing what phase you are in and what the associated objectives are. Hence it will be far easier to analyze the problem and devise a solution.

VARIATIONS ON A THEME

The J Curve's phases aren't absolute; it's possible that your start-up may not follow each phase exactly. As you are probably all too well aware, anarchy can reign during entrepreneurial ventures. At times, so much craziness happens that you don't know which way is up, let alone which phase you're in.

Recognize, therefore, that you may be out of sync with the J Curve for a few different reasons. It's possible that things are moving so fast and chaotically that the phases are blending together, and it's difficult to see the borders dividing one phase from another.

It's also possible that events are moving at a snail's pace or slower and you're stuck in a particular phase. It may take months, even years, before you can extricate yourself from whatever morass you're in and get back solidly on the J Curve path so you can start definitively moving through the phases in the proper sequential order. I have also seen situations where a company got ahead of itself and then had to back up to a previous phase and finish it properly before refocusing on growth.

But two additional factors may cause an apparent misalignment between your start-up and the phases. First, your company may have a de facto business model from its inception. Instead of waiting to create this model in a later phase, you know with a reasonable degree of certainty how the company will be structured because everyone in your field has the same basic model. Let's say you plan on launching a newspaper or magazine (a truly entrepreneurial endeavor in this digital day and age). Given models used in the past, you're likely going to have one of two revenue models—subscription based or advertising based. While you're going to have to make other decisions related to either of these models later on (i.e., how many ads per page), you have a pretty good idea of your model earlier than the J Curve suggests.

Second, you may convince yourself that you have to harvest before you scale. In the heat of the entrepreneurial moment, this may seem to make sense. Having slogged through the dip in the J Curve—the cold, dark winter of the entrepreneurial soul—you may be ready to take the first exit that presents itself (though I will try to convince you otherwise). If your finances are stretched to the max and you're physically and emotionally exhausted from trying to get your company off the ground, you may take the first buyout offer regardless of whether it's a good deal or whether it optimizes the return on the time and effort that you've put in. From your perspective, you lack the willingness and energy to go through the Scale phase and get to the Harvest phase. It seems like it's now or never (even though it probably isn't).

Given all this, it's best to treat the J Curve as a guide rather than as a bible. Or, to use another analogy, it functions much like gravity. Sooner or later, the line of the J Curve will pull a start-up toward it.

HOW YOU'LL BENEFIT

When I was contemplating writing this book, I researched the space to see what other literature was out there that could be useful to entrepreneurs and I was surprised by the paucity of it: It's a pretty thin section at the bookstore. To be sure, there are some good reads available. Peter Thiel's book *Zero to One* has, among other insights, accurate (even if politically incorrect) comments on competition. Ben Horowitz's book *The Hard Thing About Hard Things* has some great lessons about the difficulties of start-ups. Other books on the subject, like Eric Ries's *Lean Startup,* and *The Startup Playbook* by David Kidder, provide useful insights. The former stresses the importance of being fiscally conservative, learning from experience, and being sufficiently agile to respond to what's learned. The latter offers a range of entrepreneurial stories, each with its own lesson. Geoffrey Moore's book, *Crossing the Chasm,* is a start-up classic. Paul Graham's essays on start-ups are incredibly good, as is the Startup Playbook blog by Sam Altman. By all means, I encourage you to read all of these authors and more. But what I have not seen available— and what this book provides—is a start-to-finish map and a series of succinct ordered steps that will give you the best possible odds of success.

Entrepreneurs are like travelers in unexplored territory. It's easy to lose your way or to reach a crossroads and not be sure which way to go. The J Curve helps you know the best course of action at a given moment in the life of your start-up. As a result, you gain three key benefits:

- Speed. Entrepreneurs spend hours, days, and weeks engaging in premature activities (i.e., trying to grow the business before they've found the right iteration of their product). By using the J Curve, you know what you're supposed to be doing when. This helps you focus on the tasks at hand and move quickly toward goals.

- Efficiency. As you may have discovered, a huge amount of time is wasted on start-ups. And time does indeed equal money, especially in start-ups. People spend a great deal of time on unnecessary or secondary tasks. They also get side-tracked by "opportunities" that turn out to be dead ends. This is a huge problem in the resource-scarce environment of a start-up. The J Curve helps you conserve time and energy, addressing mission-critical issues in every phase and ignoring what's superfluous or what can be better addressed later.

- Confidence. More than anything else, this six-phase model allows you to make moves that are appropriate for your start-up stage. Even the most outwardly confident entrepreneurs can be plagued by doubt and uncertainty. Being in uncharted territory has that effect on people. With a map in hand, however, you can move forward knowing that you're doing the right thing.

Before moving on to an in-depth look at the J Curve's first phase, I'd like you to consider a list of the most common mistakes entrepreneurs make as they launch, build, and sustain their start-ups. Perhaps you've made some of these errors in the past. Perhaps you weren't even aware they were errors. Whatever the case, start-ups are vulnerable to all of the following mistakes, and as you'll discover, you can avoid or overcome them through an understanding of the J Curve:

- Coming up with a great start-up idea and moving forward certain that the idea alone will make you rich

- Not choosing your cofounders wisely

- Raising money from the wrong sources

- Spending too much money too quickly after initial product success

- Underestimating the amount of money you want to raise at the very beginning

- Taking too long to release your product

- Failing to listen closely to what the market is saying or doing relative to your product

- Falling victim to love-is-blind syndrome—refusing to change anything about your beloved product despite negative data

- Refusing to create a series of iterations based on customer feedback

- Keeping your initial success a secret out of fear that you'll give competitors an edge

- Accepting a lowball offer as your company begins to grow

- Scaling before nailing the business model

- Not getting the right people with the right skills into specialized roles required for scaling

- Being unable or unwilling to make the hard decisions about how to maximize the return on your start-up

CREATE

Create

2

CREATE:
TEMPER DREAMS WITH IDEAS,
MONEY, STRUCTURE, AND TEAMS

The Create phase is the time when everything seems possible to ambitious entrepreneurs. In phase 1 of the J Curve, start-ups are in their infancy, but their founders are fueled by big dreams; they don't know all the obstacles that lay ahead or how difficult the journey can be. Most are a bit naive when they create their start-up, but this naïveté allows them to push forward despite the unknowns and tough odds that lay ahead.

Unbridled optimism is great, but don't let it interfere with start-up realities. Getting off on the right foot increases the odds of a start-up's success.

Therefore, let's look at the key activities in this first phase as well as mistakes and misconceptions that can stand in the way of a strong start. We'll examine how to create the right team, structure the enterprise properly, and raise money, but all of these actions will matter little without a good approach to your initial idea.

THE DIRTY LITTLE SECRET OF GREAT IDEAS

Many people—especially many neophyte entrepreneurs—believe that the idea is everything. The assumption is that if you possess a great idea, the world will beat a path to your door, your start-up will soar, and you will soon be on the sandy beach of your tropical island counting your cash.

Not necessarily. In fact, my partner, David, and I estimate that the initial idea's value to a start-up is approximately 5 percent—and that number may be high. The value of the idea is low for two reasons: (1) The vast majority of initial ideas don't work out as originally envisioned, and (2) no start-up succeeds without a massive amount of nuts-and-bolts, grind-it-out execution. With mediocre or poor execution, even the best ideas are bound to fail.

Misconception about the value of an idea begins when a great product hits it big and people say, "I had that same idea years ago; if I had done something about it, I would be rich." In reality, it's not the idea that creates huge success as much as how that idea is executed.

Here's a dirty little secret about great ideas: *Many of the ideas that spawned highly successful companies didn't seem so great when these companies were in their infancy.*

A case in point is Uber. With hindsight, of course, the idea for an alternative, mobile phone–activated taxi company is brilliant. At the time, however, it seemed flawed. A friend of mine was asked to invest, and the Uber pitch was, "We are going to offer the ability to order black-car services via an app on your smart phone." But as my friend correctly perceived, numerous problems existed with this idea.

First, black-car services had been around for a hundred years and had not been a particularly good business; no national company or brand ever evolved from this fragmented marketplace. Second, traditional taxis were deeply entrenched in just about every market; it didn't appear as if there was sufficient dissatisfaction with taxis to open the door for an alternative approach. Third, at the time, Uber had a relatively high valuation of ten million dollars.

So my friend declined to invest. Within five years, Uber's valuation rose to over fifty billion dollars. What helped it become a sixty-seven-country, three-hundred-city behemoth, however, wasn't the idea itself, but the execution of the idea. Uber was aggressive and creative in recruiting drivers, iterating its app, and fending off counterstrikes by entrenched taxi companies and government bureaucracies. Uber has been accused of being "Uber-competitive," but that accusation is a testament to their ability to aggressively execute their plan quickly, thoroughly, and astutely.

Another example of a product succeeding due to superior execution, as opposed to the idea, is Dropbox. If you were to look at the current success of this company and its valuation near ten billion dollars, you might say, "Wow, genius idea! I should have thought of that!" But many people did think of it. I recall brainstorming with my friend Chris Kruse years ago, when it seemed obvious that central, cloud-based storage held many benefits. But numerous companies moved into that space before we could, and the clutter turned this type of a service into a commodity; few companies made much money. The Dropbox idea was late to the party, but what its founders figured out was that an incredibly simple product combined with great execution was a differentiator. Simplicity and execution were the keys to success, not the raw great idea.

I said this in the previous chapter, and I'll say it again here (and again later, since it's so important): The proper way to view an initial idea is as a hypothesis. It may or may not work. If it doesn't work, you will take what you learned and create something new that is more successful. If you execute this process well, then your odds of success will greatly increase. In the Create phase, therefore, you should not pursue the original great idea as if it's the Holy Grail.

On the other hand, pursuing potentially marketable ideas is essential. You don't need the next Uber to create a successful start-up, but you do need a building block to establish the foundation of your company. You have three viable options for identifying building block ideas or products.

1. A Product or Service That Solves a Problem

There are always problems to be solved, and not all of the good, problem-solving ideas have been taken. Not by a long, long, long shot. If you look creatively and perceptively at what people are concerned about in any sphere, you'll find a host of problems begging for solutions. Certainly, many tech start-ups recognize this truth— there seems to be a new, great problem-solving app born every day. But here's a classic, nontech example that demonstrates many problems still exist that are waiting for start-up solutions.

Growing up, my friends and I loved to jump on trampolines, but they were safety hazards; every so often, a kid would bounce off and over the side of a trampoline and break a leg or an arm. In 1997, after witnessing such an accident, Mark Publicover designed and built a safety net enclosure system. Such a system has become standard on every trampoline sold, reducing accidents significantly, and more to the point, Publicover built a successful business based on his product's ability to solve a problem. Just as instructive, however, is that from 1936, when the first trampoline was built, to 1997, sixty years passed. The safety net enclosure solution required no new technology; it could have been invented at any point in the preceding sixty years. It took a long time indeed for someone to recognize that people flying off trampolines was a preventable event and solve the problem with a viable product. It remains a complete mystery to me as to why this problem took so long to solve, but it's illustrative of the innumerable problems that are latent in our world and just waiting for you to solve them. Make a conscious effort to attune yourself to recognize them.

2. A Visionary, Breakthrough Product

Apple CEO Tim Cook described this type of product as "something you didn't know you wanted. And then once you got it, you can't imagine your life without it." This is a tougher path for an entrepreneur to forge, but if you manage to produce something that meets Cook's definition, then you may have a big hit on your hands. Cook knows what he's talking about, since many of the Apple products fall into this category. The iPod, for instance, didn't solve an immediate obvious problem because, at the time of its introduction, the market was flooded with relatively inexpensive MP3 players. But Steve Jobs had a breakthrough vision—a series of hardware and software products linked together in the music delivery chain, where people could seamlessly buy music, download it onto their computer, and play it on their iPod. At the time, people didn't know they wanted an iPod and probably weren't sure they wanted to pay for music. Even music industry executives were highly uncertain as to whether they wanted to participate in Jobs's proposed scheme, and many initially refused. But Jobs's vision was accurate and soon became their reality. Shortly after the iPod's release, music lovers discovered they couldn't do without the iPod.

Facebook is another example of a product that didn't solve an obviously existing problem but was driven by a vision. As many Facebook addicts will attest, they can't imagine life without it.

Being a visionary doesn't come cheap. If you're contemplating a visionary product idea, you often need a sizable investment—more than the typical problem-solving product. On the plus side, these types of ideas often have larger outcomes, and as such, they appeal to venture capital firms (VCs). The VCs tend to gravitate toward businesses with boom-or-bust outcomes that either work in a big way or fail. They require a small number of big hits, and they are drawn to visions. The bad news is that the failure rate is higher for this category than the previous one, so you need to have a tolerance for risk if you're pursuing something in this area.

3. An Opportunistic Product

While opportunistic product ideas may possess elements of the previous two groups, they are distinguished by timely events and circumstances that represent opportunities; these opportunities act as catalysts for entrepreneurial start-ups. In the late nineties, people began to realize that a large swath of corporate software would stop working in the year 2000 because, in computer code, the year was often represented with two digits; the fear was that the year 2000 would be mistaken as 1900. Referred to as the Y2K problem (for year 2000), it spawned an entire industry of consultants and products that helped companies find and fix this problem. I would term most of these businesses *opportunistic* in that the problem and demand was obvious. If you started a company that focused on that problem, you probably did OK, at least until after Y2K, after which many of the firms either folded or morphed into consulting shops to leverage their client relationships.

This type of idea carries less risk than the previous two, since some pieces are often in place before the entrepreneur becomes involved. They frequently don't require as much of an investment as some other start-ups, since some of the work has been done and the opportunity often revolves around a money-making concept. If there's a drawback to this category, it's that it's easy to overestimate the opportunity and underestimate the difficulty of capitalizing on it. These ideas tend not to be blockbusters and often end up as lifestyle businesses. You also shouldn't expect venture capital money for this type of product, since they tend to like bigger, sexier ideas rather than targeted, opportunistic ones that may have limited upside and lack strong differentiation.

At this point, you might be thinking that I've forgotten a fourth product category—technological innovation. A scientist or tech genius creates something in the lab that astonishes his colleagues. It's innovative, cutting edge, and brilliant in design. Invariably, it attracts a following, and a team comes together to market it. Unfortunately, it's technology in search of a market, and it often doesn't find one. Great technology is seductive, but it can also be illusory— it creates the illusion that tech brilliance translates directly into product sales. On occasion, this translation can occur, especially if a savvy businessperson is involved who can pry the technology out of the research lab and find marketable applications. But in most cases, it's wise to heed the voice of the tech master Steve Jobs, who in a 1997 speech at the Worldwide Developers Conference said, "You've got to start with the customer experience and work back toward the technology—not the other way around."

One great method to help surface good ideas for the Create phase is to become problem sensitive. This means training yourself to notice the problems all around you or, rather, overcoming your natural propensity to gloss over problems. We mentally fast-forward through problems as a matter of survival; if we obsess over every minor obstacle that crosses our path, we'll never accomplish anything, and we might be miserable. I'm not suggesting that you become so problem sensitive that you become incapacitated. I am suggesting that increasing this sensitivity will facilitate your search for a marketable product.

For instance, say you have to make a last-minute, inconvenient trip to the store because you've run out of razor blades. So you drag yourself out of the house late on a Sunday night, arrive at the store, find your package of eight razor blades, and buy them for $32. Right there are two big problems: inconvenience and cost.

The guys who started the $1 Shave Club were probably sensitive to these problems, and it led them to a solution: Subscribe to the club for $1, and the club sends you razor blades monthly. It's a simple but brilliant problem-solving idea, and it hooked me. Their costs of manufacture and shipping are low, and they also upsell you to fancier blades, resulting in even more profit. As the club's motto goes, "Shave time, shave money."

By paying close attention to problems in your life—when you shop, at work, when you're online—you can find potential ideas for start-ups. On top of that, you can determine if a problem is significant and widespread (rather than minor and a result of your own idiosyncrasies) by talking to others. Are your friends and colleagues as irritated as you are by a given problem? If so and if you think it's a problem you can solve, you may want to move forward on creating a solution. And this is a much better approach than the typical brainstorming sessions that some start-up aspirants favor—in which people throw out all sorts of imaginative concepts that sound good in the conference room but lack a real-world foundation and customer resonance, like having to go out to the store for an overpriced package of razor blades.

I recognize that looking for problems may sound simplistic from an idea-generation standpoint. Obviously, it takes more than the recognition that gasoline is too expensive to develop a marketable alternative fuel. At the same time, don't be daunted by big problems. Elon Musk was determined to tackle our dependence on fossil fuels, and his boldness has led him to create Tesla and Solar City. Training yourself to recognize the problems in life is a great start, but don't stop there. Be creative in coming up with solutions, and then figure out a way to make your solution a reality and a viable business.

You also need to ask yourself if you're passionate about the given problem and solution. Passion is a key ingredient and will help you overcome the many hurdles a start-up presents. Start-ups are incredibly hard, and if you aren't fully engaged in what you're doing, then you have a problem you can't solve.

Numerous factors affect whether a start-up idea bears fruit, but the genesis is often some problem that bothers you or inspires you—a problem that an observant entrepreneur grasps and responds to before their potential competitors, who are still in their conference room brainstorming.

BUT WHAT ABOUT THE MARKET?

Before moving on to the structure requirements of the Create phase, I should note that many advisers suggest that it's crucial for entrepreneurs to determine their market size as soon as possible. In fact, though, many savvy entrepreneurs start with a narrow idea, but once they gain traction with customers, they expand their market. Amazon started with the narrow market of book buyers, and many observers were aghast at its high stock price when it went public; it was only a bookseller, after all. You could have almost gotten in a fistfight trying to defend Amazon's market capitalization. I kept hearing, "Amazon has a higher market cap than all of the booksellers combined!" But after they gained traction in books, they soon expanded into CDs, then DVDs, and before long, they were selling washing machines. I can't think of much they don't sell at this point, including cloud-based web services that most of my companies use. Great entrepreneurs and great companies will keep redefining themselves as they push into new markets.

Yes, venture capital firms want you to define the total addressable market (TAM), and they want that market to be big. Yes, many start-up presentations include a slide that reads *Really Big Opportunity*. But in the early stage of a start-up, it can be difficult to make a credible case for that really big market, and it may not be advisable because going after too large a market may diffuse your focus. So while it's a worthy exercise to consider the total addressable market, I try not to get too caught up in it when I am hearing a start-up pitch.

STRUCTURE: BUILDING A BETTER START-UP

This is your opportunity to create the building blocks of your evolving company—blocks that should fit well with your idea. These foundational elements may change a bit as the start-up evolves through its other phases, but they provide a basis for moving forward, so it's wise to get them right. These three elements are the following:

- corporation type,
- business plan or pitch deck, and
- team.

The first one is the most prosaic, and I'm not going to go into great detail about all the implications of various legal corporate structures; I recommend that you consult with a good attorney to make these assessments. But you should know the main structures you have to choose from—DBA, LLC, S corporation, and C corporation. Here is a snapshot of their pros and cons:

- **DBA.** This one is quick, easy, and inexpensive to set up, but it provides scant legal protection and doesn't allow for outside investment. This can be a good placeholder for the earliest stages, but if you want legal protection and are going to raise any money, this won't work.

- **LLC and S Corporation.** These are often overlooked, and I see people choose C corporations reflexively without considering these. But in certain situations they can offer big advantages. I'm discussing these two together because they both offer tax advantages to start-ups with cash flow; excess cash isn't taxed at the corporate level prior to being distributed. They also allow you to deduct early losses on your personal income tax. While they are more expensive than a DBA, they are often the optimal structure for start-ups that have good potential for generating cash, and David and I use them regularly. Also, if you decide later on that a C corp will suit you better, it is usually possible to convert into one (consult a good attorney).

- **C Corporation.** Venture capital firms require these structures for the start-ups they fund, so they are best suited for companies that are raising significant funds. They are also well suited for capitalizing on certain types of tax breaks, such as the qualified small business stock (QSBS), which make reduced capital gains rates possible in certain circumstances.

Again, I encourage you to spend time up front discussing these options thoroughly with your lawyer and accountant and considering all the facts and circumstances relative to you and your start-up.

Now, let's move on to the second structural element: business plans or pitch decks. Up until the mid-nineties, you needed a detailed business plan if you wanted to raise money for your venture. These plans were often gargantuan, as if the sheer volume of pages might convince an investor that a start-up concept was viable. Fortunately, both entrepreneurs and financial backers recognized that they were counterproductive. Too often, they locked start-ups into an inflexible business plan that was ill suited to the company's evolution. Instead of being agile and stretching and growing as a product morphed, these companies stuck by their business plans and sometimes went under because of them.

The simpler PowerPoint pitch deck presentations eventually took over, and they are a significant improvement on epic business plans. Typically, each slide focuses on a business issue, ensuring a concise presentation. Unlike the business plan approach, these presentations leave sufficient room to deviate from the core strategy if circumstances dictate changes. While you can create these presentations in many different ways, you might consider the model established by venture firm Sequoia Capital, which suggests fifteen to twenty slides in the following sequence: company purpose, problem, solution, why now, market size, competition, product, business model, team, financials. Kevin Hale from Y Combinator also has a good post about creating a more effective pitch deck, where he stresses the basics: Make it simple, make it legible, and make it obvious. I agree completely; simplicity always trumps complexity—as my friend and master salesman Lance Black is fond of saying, "A confused mind always says no!" Legible means what it says, that you choose the right-sized fonts and contrasting colors. I see decks all the time where I have to squint. To see your funding prospect squinting at your deck is not a good thing. Obvious means that the slide(s) can be understood at a glance. Overall, having a great deck is not going to take you much more time, and it's going to give you a lot of confidence when you make your presentations. It's also going to give you a much higher success rate on getting to the next stage of your funding discussions.

To give you a better sense of what an effective pitch looks like, here's the presentation from Elli, one of my start-ups:

ELLI BUSINESS PLAN

The company purpose is pretty straightforward: "Style your wedding."

THE PROBLEM

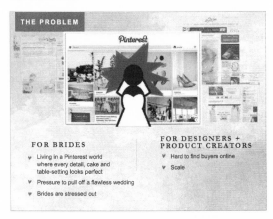

The slide points out that the bar for perfect weddings keeps rising, and brides feel incredible pressure to deliver, but they don't have the time, money, and resources.

THE SOLUTION

The Elli solution is credibly presented.

MARKET SIZE

The market for wedding-related products is darn big. Anyone with a daughter knows that the cost of weddings is a major life expense.

THE COMPETITION

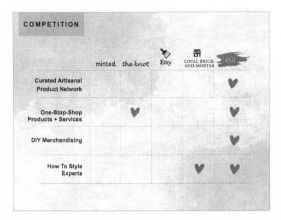

I am often skeptical of these competition slides because they tend to be quite biased, but it's a good starting point for the competitive discussion.

BUSINESS MODEL

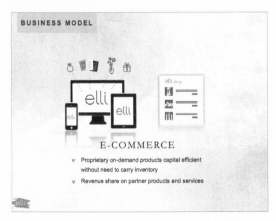

This clearly states the e-commerce business model, without the need to carry inventory.

WHAT WE'RE DOING NOW

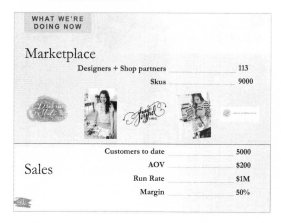

WHAT WE'RE DOING NOW

Marketplace

Designers + Shop partners	113
Skus	9000

Sales

Customers to date	5000
AOV	$200
Run Rate	$1M
Margin	50%

This shows the current state of the business and the key performance metrics.

THE LIFETIME VALUE

CUSTOMER ACQUISITION

Lifetime Value 3.1X Customer Acquisition Cost

	Marketplace in Development	Full Marketplace + Services
Number of US weddings annually	2,000,000	2,000,000
Ell market share	0.22%	10%
Customers	4,433	200,000
AOV	$205	$150
Purchases per year	2	4
Avg. customer lifespan (yrs)	1.5	1.5
Lifetime revenue per customer	$615	$900
Revenue	$2,726,295	$180,000,000
Margin	50%	50%
Gross margin per customer	$307.50	$450.00
CAC	$75.00	$50.00
Lifetime value per customer	$232.50	$400.00

This shows the assumptions behind the key elements of the business model.

RECOUPING

CUSTOMER ACQUISITION

Recouping 2X CAC on First Purchase
through Paid Marketing Channels

	Facebook	Blended Paid Channels
CAC	$110.00	$75.00
AOV	$250.00	$205.00
Gross margin	$137.50	$112.75
Marketing cost	$110.00	$75.00
Contribution	$27.50	$37.75
Contribution % of sales	11%	18%

This slide shows the return on marketing dollars, which is a critical element of this business.

LEVERAGE ACCOMPLISHMENTS

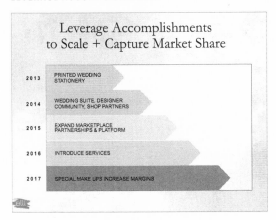

This slide details the product roadmap.

THE TEAM

The team slide shows the current state of the key management roles.

THE BUDGET

	2015	2016	2017	2018	2019	2020
FINANCIALS						
Orders	6,250	15,000	45,000	175,000	400,000	700,000
AOV	$200	$200	$175	$150	$150	$150
Revenue	$1,250,000	$3,000,000	$7,875,000	$26,250,000	$60,000,000	$105,000,000
COGS	$625,000	$1,500,000	$4,331,250	$15,750,000	$36,000,000	$63,000,000
Gross Margin	50%	50%	45%	40%	40%	40%
Expense	$800,000	$1,300,000	$1,600,000	$7,500,000	$10,000,000	$20,000,000
Net Margin	-$175,000	$200,000	$1,943,750	$3,000,000	$14,000,000	$22,000,000

This shows the actual and projected budget.

FINANCIAL PROJECTION

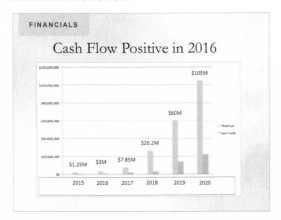

This shows the proverbial "up and to the right" projections, which I usually ignore.

Finally, let's look to how you build your founding team. I'm not going to get into a discussion of employee-hiring best practices, aside from suggesting that you bring on people who not only have complementary skills but passion, integrity, and commitment. Instead, I'd like you to consider whether you're going to go it alone as a founder, or bring in one or more cofounders. Certainly, there are single entrepreneurs who have been highly successful with their start-ups—Amazon's Jeff Bezos is a prominent example—but generally speaking, cofounders have advantages that single founders lack.

Think about some of the most successful cofounders: Apple's Steve Jobs and Steve Wozniak, Microsoft's Bill Gates and Paul Allen (and later Steve Ballmer), Google's Sergey Brin and Larry Page, Yahoo's Jerry Yang and Dave Filo. I originally thought Larry Ellison was an example of a single founder, until my friend Kip Sheeline reminded me that indeed he had two cofounders, Bob Miner and Ed Oates. A synergy exists between cofounders with similar visions but different talents—a synergy that you can't approximate on your own. More specifically, here are two advantages of having a good cofounder:

They facilitate getting through the tough times. There will be tough times, and it's good to have a wingman. To overcome obstacles, it helps to have a partner with whom you can share your concerns and hammer out critical strategies and decisions. You'll likely have a few heated discussions or arguments, but you'll likely end up with a better product and better decisions because of them. In addition, a cofounder should help you be more intellectually honest, a huge saver of time. If you're honest about a product, market, or people that aren't working out, you'll be quicker to react and address it.

Cofounders provide complementary skills or areas of knowledge. As skilled and smart as you may be, you probably lack expertise and experience in certain spheres. A cofounder who can supply the complementary knowledge and skill sets that you lack is invaluable, and not only because you don't have to hire someone to take on these tasks. The aforementioned synergies result when two individuals with complementary skills are committed to a common vision and work together to achieve far more than they could have individually.

Choosing a cofounder can be a bit tricky, because besides complementary skills, you should also seek someone who wants to do tasks you don't want to do (and vice versa) and is particularly skilled at them. In many cofounding situations, one partner will handle the customer-facing tasks, such as sales, marketing, business development, PR, and fund-raising, while the other founder takes on technology responsibilities associated with development of the product or service. In addition, it's ideal to choose someone with whom you've worked before and where mutual respect and trust already exists. This individual isn't always easy to find; you should consider people with whom you've watched and interacted with in work situations or even went to school with. A shared history and the ability to work well with someone can go a long way toward ensuring a stable and fruitful collaboration.

RAISING MONEY

Raising money is the sine qua non of phase 1. Until you generate a positive cash flow, your start-up will need to raise adequate funding, or it will sputter and eventually die. As obvious as this may be, many entrepreneurs make the mistake of raising too few dollars initially on the assumption that it will be easier to raise money later; they assume that once they have the company up and rolling, the money will pour in. In fact, at the beginning of your venture, you're selling a vision and long-term dream, and those attract more money than the coming harsh realities. Once you've launched your product, investors will be inclined to take a wait-and-see attitude; they will scrutinize everything, including customer traction, customer acquisition, expected value of a customer, and product reviews. Any glitch during the launch can make an investor hesitant to give you money, so it's best to raise as much money as possible as soon as possible.

Recognize, too, that entrepreneurs often underestimate two things: how quickly they will burn through the money they do raise and how long it will take them to reach future milestones that are significant enough to justify a meaningfully higher valuation.

At this point in our conversation with entrepreneurs, some of them will bring up the subject of dilution. Specifically, they're concerned about diminishing their ownership stake in the company by giving away pieces of the enterprise to investors. No doubt, someone has warned them of the dangers of dilution. The truth is that the start-up founders' stake in the company diminishes from day one; it's simply the cost of doing business. While dilution reduces your share of the company, the additional funds increase your odds of making it successful, so the result is that your remaining shares should go up in value. So you should focus on what your holdings are worth, not the percentage of the company you own. More important than dilution or even the actual money is the value-add potential of the investor; a seasoned start-up investor can make a big difference. I've had the privilege of working with some extraordinary investors who consistently add a tremendous amount of value. I've also had to deal with a few folks who are a net negative. So seek investors with as much value add as possible. If you need to give them a deal to be on board, do it! Now, let's look at the three potential sources of investment dollars, and the pros and cons of each:

Friends and Family

Though you may be reluctant to ask people close to you for money, keep an open mind about it. It's usually the easiest way to obtain at first. In the majority of start-ups, these individuals provide at least part of the initial funding. While your reluctance is understandable—you don't want to mix the personal and the professional parts of your life—it may also prevent you from capitalizing on a key funding source. As much as you may fear that you'll ruin a relationship because your start-up failed to give someone the return he expected, if they indicate an interest, I would not deny them the opportunity. I've regularly invested in friends and have lost money occasionally. After an awkward week or so, you get back to being friends. My own feeling is that, from an investor's perspective, the only thing worse than investing in friends and losing money is *not* investing in friends and having them hit it out of the park. That's the worst of all worlds, because not only did you not back your buddy, but you missed a great opportunity to make money and have a fun ride.

I don't have the perfect solution to the awkwardness of raising money through family and friends, but here are a few quick tips to protect the relationship if you decide to go that route. First, communicate clearly that it's possible the venture will fail and that they may lose all of the money they invested. Second, tell them to limit their investment to what they can afford to lose. Third, give them a generous deal, so that they will be especially well compensated for the risk they are taking. This group is typically not sophisticated with respect to valuations or inclined to argue them, so it's your responsibility to give them a good deal. This is also a highly motivating funding strategy. You will feel a special obligation not to let these people down, and that should motivate you to work harder and smarter. When the chips are down, the best entrepreneurs will move heaven and earth to avoid losing money for those with whom they have a close relationship.

Especially if you're a first-time entrepreneur, this is the easiest money to obtain—and it's often the only money available, so don't dismiss this possible funding source reflexively.

Angel Investors

Angel investors are a varied group (of which I am a member), though many angels are successful business executives and entrepreneurs who have started and run their own companies. Some are dabblers, making infrequent investments, while others are full-time investors and may invest in a dozen or more enterprises annually. More selective than friends and family, angel investors will do more analysis before committing funds. They usually invest in the early stages of a venture—like our phase 1 and 3—and they also tend to negotiate terms that will meet their requirements.

To entice angels, you will usually need a prototype or minimum viable product, which is referred to commonly as an MVP. Angels don't invest as a fund (the way venture capitalists do); they are usually relatively flexible about their investment time horizon and how you run and evolve the company.

Another benefit is that many angel investors can add real value by providing advice or mentoring. Unless you've done start-ups a few times before, you can improve your success rate and make the journey more enjoyable if you have some solid outside mentors to help you; these mentors often provide great assistance even when founders have lots of start-up experience. Not all angel investors want to take on this mentoring role, of course, and prefer to drop off the check and have limited additional responsibility. This type of angel investor is involved in spray and pray: They place a large number of relatively small bets on the theory that a few will work out well. Others will have a more concentrated portfolio with larger individual investments, and they expect to do everything they can to make sure the enterprise has the best chance of success, including providing mentorship.

Venture Capital

I believe that the ideal use for traditional venture capital, or what we often call Sand Hill money (named after the road in Menlo Park where so many venture firms are located), is for scaling a business (phase 5). I think prior to that it's a bit of a toss up: It can be useful or it can be a hindrance, depending on the VC involved and the evolution of the company. But once you get to phase 5 (Scale), there is no better funding source than venture capital and the people that go with it. As we will see in more detail later in the book, scaling requires people, process, and money. Venture capitalists (at least the ones I know) are extraordinarily good at all three of those.

It's worth saying up front that venture capital money is incredibly difficult to obtain, and it is not designed for every start-up.

In fact, many of you may want to avoid this route altogether. It's great for companies with visionary, breakthrough ideas that need to rapidly scale up. Venture firms typically invest in the later stages and can write far larger checks than angel investors. They have great contacts and can provide perceptive operational and financial advice. In the handful of situations that venture capitalists have been investors in our companies, they have been great partners. But the odds are that your start-up won't qualify for venture capital funds because venture capitalists are highly selective and also tend to limit themselves to a specific type of company that fits their business model. This model depends on a small number of large winners. Specifically, these firms are looking for what are known as *unicorns*—the one company out of the thirty or so that can become worth a billion dollars or so and return the total value of their fund all by itself. If a venture capital fund is $300 million, for instance, then a start-up that receives $10 million needs to grow at least thirty times the investment to equal the fund total. To achieve that growth, venture capital investors can sometimes put pressure on companies to get big fast. This is fine if it works, but it carries a lot of risk because in many cases the imperative to get big can be inappropriate or premature. Put another way, venture capital funds can't typically survive on a company that is only growing at 20 to 40 percent. On the other hand, you can get rich from those kinds of growth rates over time. So, while venture capital funds can be useful for companies that need to scale rapidly, many start-ups and their founders aren't well suited for the venture capital business model.

Without the large influx of dollars that venture capital provides, start-ups must reach profitability quickly so they can bootstrap their way to additional growth. This may seem like a negative, but in my experience, it imposes a useful discipline on the venture. It helps entrepreneurs nail their business models and adopt good habits that will serve them well as they move forward.

EXAMINE YOUR ATTITUDE

It's not just what you do in the Create phase that counts but your attitude about the business. Remember, entrepreneurs possess dreams unburdened by reality. While this may cause you to make head-in-the-clouds mistakes, it also provides you with a significant benefit. It's like a couple before they have their first child; they blissfully have no idea what they're getting into.

For first-time entrepreneurs (like first-time parents), this naïveté can help you move forward inspired, rather than anticipating the worst. More specifically for entrepreneurs, unbridled optimism confers two benefits in the Create phase:

1. Since you don't know how difficult start-ups can be, you're better able to move boldly forward without too much second-guessing, hesitation, and paralysis.

2. Your naive mind protects you from the ossified mentality of those who accept the status quo. In short, you are less inclined to accept the world as it is and more open to opportunities to change it for the better.

These benefits will help you find solutions that a more experienced, more cynical entrepreneur may not find. Start-ups thrive on unconventional thinking. They need founders who refuse to give up and who won't let an obstacle stop them in their tracks.

At the same time, neophyte entrepreneurs should be wary of

how their naïveté may cause them to fall madly and inflexibly in love with their idea during the Create phase. Most start-ups succeed only after going through a series of fundamental variations on the initial idea; the idea that eventually carries the business into profitability and growth usually bears little resemblance to the original concept. By embracing this reality in the early phase of your start-up, you may save yourself a lot of headaches, not to mention saving the business.

The operative paradox here is that you must take your idea seriously, but not too seriously. This means working hard to come up with a great product or service and doing everything possible to make it successful. Simultaneously, recognize that you may have to let go of this original idea at some point. I realize that this again recalls our parent-child analogy; love your kid, but be prepared to let him go and do her own thing.

What may help you manage the paradox is thinking about your start-up idea as a hypothesis. You'll develop, test, and implement the hypothesis, but be prepared to find a flaw in it. The hypothesis, flawed though it may be, serves a purpose because it may lead to the discovery of a successful product, albeit in a different form. Time is of the essence, so you want to possess the capacity to jettison significant portions of the original idea and move on to the next iteration. Your commitment to making progress rather than to a specific product is what's important.

Embrace the unknown is a good adage to work by. Most of us like logical, predicable environments, so this advice isn't always easy to follow. But if you fool yourself—if you pretend as if your start-up journey is logical and predictable—you're going to be blindsided. Therefore, it's better to accept the unknown. You're likely to encounter both good and bad situations that come out of left field, and your well-laid plans will need to be significantly altered. If you can develop this attitude, you'll have a tremendous advantage. Rather than panic and overreact when you're surprised by events, you can deal with them objectively and analytically.

When you embrace the unknown, you also guard against hubris. Well-placed confidence is good for a start-up, but hubris is toxic. In the Create phase, some entrepreneurs are so bullish about their companies and ideas that they find it impossible to consider alternatives. They are so locked into their plans and goals that they can't deviate from them, even when the marketplace is telling them to deviate. Embracing the unknown can help you stay on the right side of the hubris–confidence line. When you accept that your start-up is no more than a working hypothesis and that unexpected developments can change this hypothesis, you possess the agility necessary to change.

APPEARANCES VERSUS REALITY

As founders get their companies up and running, they are often inspired by other start-up success stories. That's terrific, but many times they are trying to replicate a success story without knowing all the facts. As a result, they get off on the wrong foot during the Create phase, and it's difficult for them to get back on track.

Most people know Twitter as a runaway success, a quintessential example of a start-up that became a unicorn. But the reality is that Twitter was created as a side project in another start-up called Odeo. Odeo's original idea was a podcasting platform, but when Apple created and included its own platform in all its ten million iPods, Odeo's reason for being dimmed and just about disappeared. CEO Evan Williams encouraged his employees to come up with an alternative product idea that might save the company, and one of those employees, Jack Dorsey, proposed a product that had to do with status—a way to let others know exactly what you were doing at a given moment in time. Odeo cofounder Evan Glass eventually warmed to the idea—an idea that began as a way to text to one number and simultaneously send the message to a larger group of friends. Nonetheless, many Odeo investors were unimpressed with Twitter's initial test period—there were only five thousand registered users. So Evan Williams bought the company from investors, and shortly thereafter, the company took off. But if you think about it, the majority of Odeo was focused on podcasting, and even though Twitter seems like a no-brainer investment with hindsight, at the time, few people had the vision to see it as more than a side project.

HotelTonight is another example of a start-up that, through laser-like focus on a single idea, became a huge success. Founder Sam Shank had the idea to create a mobile app that would allow people to buy discounted hotel rooms at the last minute. I recall seeing the sketch of the idea that Sam had put on a whiteboard in a tiny, cramped office above a San Mateo bar, and it was a terrific concept (and this original whiteboard now is on display in Hotel-Tonight's sprawling San Francisco office). In four years, Sam, COO Jared Simon, and CTO Chris Bailey built an amazing company that came to dominate last-minute hotel bookings.

What most people don't know, however, is that HotelTonight was a spinout from another company called DealBase, which David and I helped Sam start two years before the inception of HotelTo-night. DealBase was designed to help travelers find great hotel deals. Sam and his team did an excellent job of building that business, and it still exists today. Sam astutely recognized the potentially larger opportunity in mobile bookings and quickly pursued it.

The lesson: Be cautious about the romantic stories of one-way, instant start-up success. If you dig into the reality of those stories, you'll often find a messy beginning. In the Create phase especially, entrepreneurs are looking for successful models to replicate. That's fine, but recognize that you may be following an incomplete or imperfect model. Start-ups zig and zag; they are a journey, not a destination.

BUILDING THE INITIAL PRODUCT

Once you've decided on what you want your initial product to be, test that hypothesis to see if it's valid, to see if you have something that people want. First, you should realize that one way to test the hypothesis is not to build the product at all, but simply to talk to people (preferably potential customers) and see if they do indeed want it. Talk to potential suppliers and see if you will be able to get what you need to make it. If those conversations go well, then you will want to build enough of the product to give the hypothesis a fair, real-world test. Having an actual product will, of course, provide a more valid test. But since it's still only a hypothesis, albeit backed by positive feedback, you only need enough of a product to prove the hypothesis, which is the purpose of the minimum viable product (MVP). This may seem like an overly modest goal, but it's appropriate for the Create phase. The key in this phase is to start the real customer feedback loop as quickly as possible, to discover if anyone cares and how you might need to change your product so it meets customer needs better.

Originally, Groupon was called The Point, which was a social media platform designed to facilitate collaboration among groups of people and make the world a better place. When CEO Eric Lefkofsky noticed that one group organized for the purpose of bundling their buying power to save money, he wondered if that could be a better concept than their original idea. After convincing the rest of his team that it was better, they put up a WordPress blog, started displaying daily deals, and began sending PDF coupons to their mail list. Their first deal was for two-for-one pizza at the Motel Bar, which was downstairs from The Point offices in Chicago. They didn't possess a full-blown system, and they lacked an integrated back-end, email, and other infrastructure. They cobbled the MVP together (in days, not weeks) and got it out there. The strong response they received told them they were onto something big—much bigger than The Point.

Kickstarter is an alternate funding source, mostly for things, not services, but if your product fits, it offers another way of achieving the same hypothesis-validating goal. At Kickstarter, you post the pitch for your product, complete with photos or a video of your prototype, and people can sign up to buy it. Their credit cards are charged only if enough people sign up to purchase. So it's potentially a great way to try out a pitch and see how it resonates—as well as a source of initial funding.

In your initial product spec, before you start building anything, keep asking yourself what exactly you are trying to test and what is the minimum you need to give that hypothesis a valid shot. Spending this time up front can save you from wasting a huge amount of time and money, building things that nobody cares about.

THE CREATE PHASE CHECKLIST

To facilitate your ability to move through this first start-up phase effectively, here are a series of questions that will help you assess your progress:

- Have you disabused yourself of the notion that you can't get started until you've found the perfect idea?

- Are you able to identify the type of idea and opportunity you wish to pursue: problem solving, visionary or breakthrough, opportunistic?

- Have you developed a problem consciousness? Are you on the alert for solutions to significant problems in different work spheres?

- Have you assessed different types of corporate structures and figured out which is best for your start-up?

- Have you developed a concise but comprehensive pitch deck based on the Sequoia format?

- Given your abilities and limitations, would your start-up be best served by recruiting a cofounder? If so, have you made the effort to find this individual?

- In your fund-raising goals, have you given yourself a cushion? Based on what you estimate you require financially, have you increased that amount by 50 to 100 percent?

- Are you reluctant to bring in investors or ask them to give you as much money as you need because you fear diluting your stake in the company? Can you see past this fear to the larger goal of creating a company with excellent value?

- Have you assessed the pros and cons of raising funds from friends or family, angel investors, and venture capital? Have you pursued a fund-raising strategy that is aligned with your start-up's requirements?

- Do you possess a good start-up attitude? Are you able to be confident but flexible and open to the reality that your initial idea may not be the final idea?

RELEASE

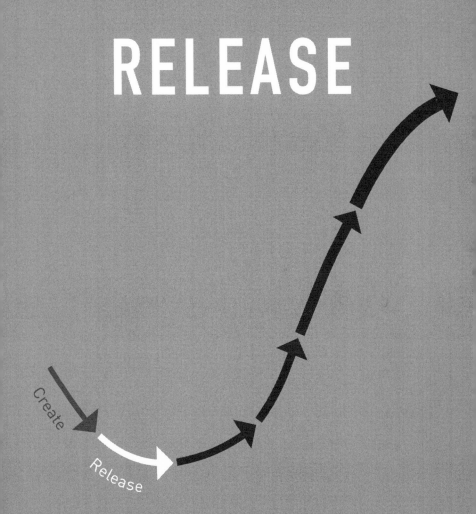

Create

Release

3

RELEASE:
GET THE DAMN THING OUT THERE

Putting your product in the customer's hands for the first time can be a challenge in more ways than one. Certainly, the tasks required to create a product and get it ready for the market require time and effort, and all sorts of logistical problems can arise that slow or stop the process—problems that most entrepreneurs solve relatively quickly, and then they move forward. But more insidious issues exist that can delay getting the product into customers' hands. Many times, these issues are self-created obstacles; start-up founders refuse to release their products until they add one more feature, or they become psychologically unable to pull the trigger.

By and large, entrepreneurs are bold risk takers who want nothing more than to bring their product idea to life. However, they are often the cause of many of the product release delays or related snafus. Consciously or not, they try to make the release perfect—a bad idea for a number of reasons.

In this second phase, push yourself and your team to get your product out into the marketplace. To facilitate this push, let's look at some of the most common reasons start-ups struggle to release products quickly.

PRACTICAL AND PSYCHOLOGICAL BLOCKS

Yes, valid reasons may exist for delaying a product release. If your competition brings out an almost identical new product one week prior to your introduction, you may need to rethink your idea or approach. If the money you were counting on to move forward suddenly dries up, you may have to wait until you can secure a new funding source. If your product is technologically challenging, you may have to put everything on hold until you get all the bugs out and can release a product that works.

You can avoid many delays, however, by distinguishing legitimate reasons to wait from minor ones or ones that are largely self-created. More product release dates can be hit if the team is solid and there is discipline around the product spec.

To that end, here are the practical and psychological causes for unnecessary release delays:

Practical Blocks
Not Embracing MVP
The first goal of the first release of a product should be a minimum viable product (MVP). The goal of an MVP is pretty simple: to test the original product hypothesis and see whether it resonates with customers. However, I often see folks treating a MVP more like the maximum value product, which has so many features, bells, and whistles that the project is tragically late to the market and collapses from its own weight.

When Lee Iacocca took over the ailing Chrysler Corporation in the early 1980s, he needed to inject new life into Chrysler's car lineup. One of his ideas was to bring back the convertible (a type of car not being offered by US companies at the time). He went to his product team and asked how long it would take to build a prototype. He was told two years, which was a problem because Chrysler would be long out of business by then. So he had his engineers take a chainsaw and welding torch to the roof of a sedan; the next day he was driving around in a convertible. As he drove around, he noticed people waving to him, smiling, and generally gawking at the top-down car. That was all the market feedback he needed. He promptly put the convertible into real production and it became a huge hit. *That* is MVP.

Lack of a Tight Product Spec
Once you have given a lot of thought to the MVP and have simplified the concept as much as possible, communicate it clearly and stick with it. There will be a lot of temptations to add features (see *feature creep* below). Those attempts need to be resisted. The only thing you should be concentrating on with respect to the spec is how to make it simpler. Deciding to throw out or delay features is fine, even advisable, if these actions will help you hit the target release date. But adding features prior to initial release almost always turns out to be a bad idea.

Unbridled Optimism
In the technology world, about 90 percent of all time estimates in the release phase are unduly optimistic. In the start-up world, the percentage is even higher. The miscalculation comes primarily in two forms: (1) Underestimating the amount of time or resources

it will take to create what is envisioned and (2) failing to factor in unforeseen technical or other challenges that are required to complete a viable product. In the Create phase, dreams are unburdened by reality, and this causes entrepreneurs to convince themselves they will be able to build their envisioned killer product in an inordinately small amount of time, everything will remain on budget, and no unexpected crises will occur. Therefore, when things don't go according to assumptions, the plan starts to come unraveled. The money raised, for example, suddenly doesn't look like enough. When you're preparing to release a product, you want to have realities unburdened by dreams—or at least be able to differentiate the two. Forcing yourself to take a hard, objective look at your situation and ensure that you are tracking to expectations—or listening to trusted advisers who help you see the realities—is a good antidote to unbridled optimism and a way to avoid the delays unwarranted optimism can cause. Successful entrepreneurs tend to be relatively honest with themselves, and this honesty saves a lot of valuable time.

Shortage of Resources

This is often a result of unbridled optimism; entrepreneurs believe they have plenty of money, employees, materials, and so on until they realize they were overly sanguine about their capacity and too grandiose in their initial product spec. A perceived shortage of resources often results from a lack of commitment to the minimum viable product. You may be giving lip service to the idea of an MVP, but if you take a hard look at the spec, there are probably features that are optional. The same holds true for expenses. If you are low on resources, it's probably because you are wasting some of those resources. When entrepreneurs discover they lack the necessary resources, they are forced to reset and cut features and expenses.

Feature Creep

You create a number of problems by adding features early on, but as you might expect, the big issue is that they each require additional time to develop and integrate into the product. You may say to yourself, "Just one more feature and we'll have it," but given that you don't know what features are most important (the marketplace will tell you after you release the product), this reason is specious. The more entrepreneurs fuss and fret over additional features, the more time is wasted with the product sitting on the shelf. Feature creep is one of the key impulses that pulls you away from a true MVP. Be vigilant for feature creep because these features really do *creep* in, one at a time. Individually, they sound innocuous, but collectively, they can be lethal.

Lack of Tight Market Definition

Start-up founders sometimes see their market as bigger and broader than it actually is, or they see what their market might become at some point in the future and go after it early in the start-up's journey. As a result, they become bogged down in trying to be all things to all people, and launching a product becomes a time-consuming, budget-destroying undertaking. Again, going for a market that is too large can tempt you away from an MVP. The more narrow a market you can define as your initial target, the more targeted your solution can be. As Sam Altman wrote: "It's much better to first make a product a small number of users love than a product that a large number of users like" (http://playbook.samaltman.com/).

Perfectionism

Sometimes, perfectionism is just an excuse to delay a product's release, and it's a seductive one, because fixing perceived or real problems feels like an essential task. But your team needs to keep things in perspective and realize that perfection isn't the goal here, but achieving a modest level of viability is. As I've emphasized, it's great to be passionate about your product and mission, but because you're dealing in a world with extremely scarce resources, you are going to be forced to make real-world tradeoffs and be more practical than perfect.

If, despite all your efforts, the product date is slipping meaningfully, start throwing features overboard. The first few that you cut from the spec will usually not matter at all, and you can always add them later.

A number of years ago, I was involved in a start-up called Green-Stack, which was designed to help people capitalize on membership discounts in a wide variety of categories. As we moved forward, we wasted an enormous amount of time trying to chase down all the discounts in all the categories. It was only in hindsight that we realized we should have limited the scope of our product and market to restaurant discounts. Ultimately, it was too late to capitalize on that understanding (there were other problems as well), and the venture didn't pan out. If we had narrowed our market definition at the start, however, we would have avoided all the wasted time and increased our chances of making the start-up a success.

Psychological Blocks
Fear of Being Judged Once the Product Hits the Market
You will be judged—the marketplace will give you a thumb's up or thumb's down. However, it shouldn't stop you from releasing your

product on a timely basis. As understandable as this fear is, move past it and recognize that judgment comes with the start-up territory and that you have to develop a thick skin. The truth is that you need that judgment in order to get a read on how your product is resonating, so don't fear it—embrace it.

Fear of Failure

An extension of the previous factor, failure is always a possibility. Indeed, your initial product release probably *will* be a failure. Get over it. You shouldn't be in the start-up business if you can't tolerate the possibility of things not working out. It's a certainty that your start-up will experience one or more small or maybe large failures on the road to success, so you have to steel yourself for these negative events.

Tinkering Syndrome

Perhaps there's a reason that many scientists struggle as start-up founders. The impulse to keep tinkering in the lab rather than releasing the product is a real problem. While I'm all for scientific discovery and the value of tinkering, I know that too much tinkering in the context of a start-up can be an unconscious delaying tactic. Tinkering may feel necessary for those of you with a lab rat's mindset, but it's a psychological crutch.

Being aware of these reasons for delay is the first step to overcoming them. Once you're conscious of your tendencies—the reasons for delay to which you're vulnerable—the easier it will be to overcome them. You should also be aware of the vague rationalizations for going slowly that run through entrepreneurial minds. Specifically, some founders delay product releases because "it isn't quite right yet." Others tell themselves they need to wait until they figure out how to monetize the product.

In terms of the former, recognize that you don't know what *right* is until you've released the product and received feedback. If the product is good enough to have a reasonable chance of success and it will test the kernel of the hypothesis, you're ready to release. In terms of the latter rationalization, it's premature to focus on the business model. At this point, just focus on making a product that people love. If you have that, then it's far easier to figure out how to make money from it.

WHAT IS A GOOD RELEASE?

Some of you may be fans of Steve Jobs and may know that he refused to release a product until he perfected it. When Apple released a product during Jobs's prime, it was often light-years ahead of the competition and made a big splash when it was introduced. But I would argue that most people aren't Steve Jobs, and their companies aren't Apple; he represented the exception rather than the rule. In fact, it can be argued that the original Apple computer was an MVP by most definitions: It was cobbled together and far from perfect.

Perfectionism has more disadvantages than advantages for most start-ups. Instead, embrace a release process that avoids perfectionism and procrastination and instead follows these steps:

1. Aim for a Minimal Viable Product (MVP)

This may seem like an overly modest goal, but it's appropriate for the release phase. In this phase, the key is to start the customer feedback loop as quickly as possible to discover how you need to change your product so it meets customer needs better. To assess whether you have an MVP, start with a hypothesis. For instance, "If we build a mousetrap that notifies you on your smart phone when the trap has caught a mouse, people will love us and pay us a lot of money for this product." You then need to ask: "What is the minimum we need to do to test and validate this hypothesis?"

The MVP might not even involve building a mousetrap. You may simply need to create a website with a compelling description of the product, generate traffic on the site, and see how many people click through to buy (letting them know when the product will be available in response).

I have seen companies bury themselves so many times, losing massive amounts of time and money, because they keep building out the product before they have proven they have something anyone cares about. They keep adding one more feature, even before they release it. The purpose of the initial product is only to prove the product hypothesis in real life, nothing more. It is an experiment. It's OK if it's a little rough; it can be rudimentary, it can be imperfect. If you are on to something special, the customers won't care. In that sense, it's almost better if the product is rough and imperfect because it will give you a more accurate signal.

2. Release It

Once your MVP is complete, you are ready to release it into the marketplace. While some businesses such as restaurants benefit from making a splash with a grand opening, this approach is usually counterproductive for start-ups. For those who are tempted to think, *If I make enough noise, people will come and buy my product, and we will be successful*, think again. In the world of start-ups, few huge launches result in hugely successful companies.

Facebook entered the world with barely a whimper; when it went live, there was no press event and no launch party. Same with Google. I assume those founders had a couple of beers and went to bed. One of my favorite start-up photographs is of Wilbur and Orville Wright at the scene of the first manned flight at Kitty Hawk, North Carolina. When you see the photograph, you can't help but be struck by how incredibly lonely it looks. There are only four people there, one of whom was thankfully a photographer. The truth is that you don't necessarily want everyone to experience your new product immediately because it probably has a long way to go before it is ready for large-scale exposure and use. It's entirely possible that it might not work. Large companies do large product launches, and that is appropriate because they have the money, the platform, prior testing, and the momentum. But a start-up is different, and in general, start-ups in the early phases are going to get into trouble when they attempt to emulate a large company. Skip the big launch and instead devote your money and time to making a product that really turns people on—so much so that they will tell their friends.

3. Focus on Initial Customer Acquisition

Obtaining customers is hard, and securing your initial customers is even harder. But the primary reason you need customers at this point is not for revenue or profit; that will come later. For now, you need customer feedback first and foremost, so do whatever is required to bring in customers for the purpose of obtaining that feedback, and be as creative as you need to be. Because these original customers aren't supposed to make the company profitable, you have great leeway to do whatever you need to do to get them, including pricing the product low or even making it available for free.

Consider following Paul Graham's advice during this phase and "do things that don't scale." For instance, the founders of Airbnb recruited customers by going from door to door in Manhattan apartment buildings. Old-fashioned, low-tech approaches are fine here. If you need to overpay for clicks via search engine marketing, that's fine too. Since you are looking for feedback, any face time you can get with customers will be invaluable. Phone calls will be helpful. If your product focus is a website and the previous suggestions are not practical, then you can run feedback surveys on your site.

4. Facilitate Feedback

Solicit feedback by communicating with customers in diverse ways—through customer surveys, as well as through in-person, phone, email, or online surveys. You don't want to just engage with your users, you want to overengage with them. Don't worry; they won't get sick of you. Most people love to provide their opinions about products, so capitalize on this tendency. The more data you acquire, the faster you'll spot the customer preference trends and be able to morph your product effectively. A tight feedback loop saves valuable time and money.

5. Listen!

Once you have some customers, listen and watch closely for what they like about your product. You are searching for whatever resonates with them. No doubt, customers will tell you what's wrong with your product; they'll tell you what features they don't like or are irrelevant to them. But it's far more important to find out what customers actually *like* about the product, no matter how small. You're going to receive a lot of data, but pay attention to these positives, because however small and seemingly trivial, they contain the clues as to what your start-up *should* be, as opposed to what its *supposed* to be. Consider what it would look like if you focused your future development efforts on the aspects of the product that people really responded to?

Steve Jobs originally conceived of the Mac as a business computer that was to compete head-to-head with the IBM PC, but this positioning didn't strike a chord with the intended market upon its release. It lacked the memory, hard drive, and software that businesses required, and most corporations preferred to stick with IBM, which was a safer choice. But what some early customers figured out was that if you combined the Mac, Apple's LaserWriter printer, and publishing software such as Aldus PageMaker, you could suddenly design, preview, and print page layouts complete with text and graphics without using an outside design shop or printer. This activity became known as desktop publishing, and it saved the Mac from becoming an epic failure. Note that Jobs did not start out by saying, "We are going to build an amazing desktop publishing computer." But it was uniquely qualified for that purpose, and Jobs was astute enough—or perhaps desperate enough—to hear that this was what customers were using it for.

When the Mac first came out, I recall that we were just about to start creating the user manual of our first product at Inmark, called Market Maker. Since I didn't code (and still don't), it fell to me to produce the user manual. So we immediately seized upon the Mac as our publishing platform, and although it was a bit slow and clunky, it did the job at a fraction of what it was going to cost to have a professional printer produce it, and we had all sorts of flexibility that a professional printer couldn't offer. The Mac was a complete flop in the primary market that Jobs and Apple intended it to compete, but it was a massive success in a use case that was barely anticipated.

As you analyze what you hear, accept that even negative feedback can be useful. Don't try to rationalize, deny, or dismiss it. Don't become discouraged and call it quits. My teenage son Peter is a soccer player and sometimes becomes upset when his coach criticizes his playing. I always remind him that his coach's criticism is a sign that the coach cares; if he were to not say anything to Peter, his silence would suggest indifference. The same lesson holds true for entrepreneurs: All feedback is valuable and should be mined for nuggets. Better that you hear that your customers hate a particular feature in the release phase than months later when you've invested a lot more time and money.

If you listen closely and pay attention to what customers care about and what they are using your product for, you can tailor your iterations astutely.

6. Keep Expenses Low

It's tough to raise funds during this phase (and will be for a while longer), so be fiscally prudent. No matter how fast you iterate, it takes time to get the product right. This is true whether your feedback is positive or negative. In the former case, don't believe you have it made and start spending like money is no longer a concern. In the latter case, don't rationalize that you have to spend money to overcome the negative initial response. That is just folly. Instead, trust in your feedback and its ability to steer you in the right product direction.

THE "ONE STEP ON THE JOURNEY" MINDSET

This isn't the make-or-break phase that many start-up founders believe it to be. Understandably, you are tremendously excited about translating your great idea into a product and seeing how customers respond. But if you view this phase as make-or-break, you'll probably be broken. The odds are that customers won't greet your product with huzzahs. The odds are that their reaction will be mixed at best.

Recognize that this phase is one step on a longer journey. Be flexible and open-minded when the feedback starts coming in, and don't be discouraged by the negatives. You may have felt you had an epiphany with your product idea in phase 1, but this is where the real epiphany happens. You obtain feedback that triggers a discussion among you and your colleagues, and you discover an opportunity that you never knew existed. You come up with an iteration—or, at least, the direction for an iteration—that you could never have come up with without releasing the original product.

In addition, recognize the advantage of bringing out your product sooner rather than later: You'll receive information critical to your next iteration faster, which means you're that much closer to a viable, money-making product. And if you have competitors, it may allow you to create this viable product before they do. Adopt a bad-news-is-good-news approach: Your product 1.0 will probably fail, but that failure will provide the information you need to create product 1.1 or 1.2 or 1.3, which will be a success. Don't get hung up on all the flaws and doubts you may have about this first version. Repeat to yourself: This is only a test. It's part of the process of producing a great product and becoming a great company.

So relax and have fun as you move into the next phase—Morph. Creativity is not often associated with entrepreneurs, but creativity is a critical component here. Be sufficiently agile so you can take the surprising data you receive and run with it in a new—or at least an alternative—direction. This is a cognitively exciting time, a puzzle to figure out and a chance to reshape a product based on real marketplace information rather than pie-in-the-sky dreams. This is your business's adolescence, so it's time to explore, to test limits, to experiment. With this mindset, you'll be well prepared to capitalize on the data you receive after your initial product release.

THE RELEASE PHASE CHECKLIST

As relatively simple as this phase may appear to be, it's a trap in waiting for unwary entrepreneurs. Here is where you can get stuck, bogged down in adding features, in fretting about minor matters that seem major, and in trying to perfect something that can't be perfected at this point. To make sure you release your product on a timely basis and in the right way, review the following checklist:

- Are your expectations realistic; are you prepared for at least some feedback that causes you to alter your product and your plans? Will you be able to overcome negative responses and continue to work toward creating a better version of your original product?

- Do you have a clear product hypothesis, and have you designed a true minimum viable product (MVP) to test its validity?

- Have you defined your product and market narrowly? Have you focused tightly on a small group of users rather than trying to appeal to a variety of audiences?

- Are you moving forward with sufficient resources? Have you accurately assessed the money and people you require to release the product effectively?

- Is feature creep delaying your product release? Do you find yourself thinking that if you add just one more feature, you can make your product a rousing success?

- Do you find yourself hesitating to release your product because you fear being criticized or of failing?

- Are you a product tinkerer; are you fussing with your product to the point that it's delaying the release date by months or longer?

- Once you've released your product, are you paying attention to what customers are telling you with an open mind? Are you attuned to what resonates with your customers?

- Are you making a concerted effort to generate customer feedback, especially if you are a small start-up operating on a limited budget? Is your product priced sufficiently low? Are you reaching out to customers through surveys and other means?

- Are you working hard to rein in expenses? Are you resisting the urge to spend in response to positive or negative feedback?

- Are you able to stay away from a make-or-break mindset during this phase? Are you able to embrace a more experimental approach in which you see the initial product release as one early step with many more to come?

MORPH

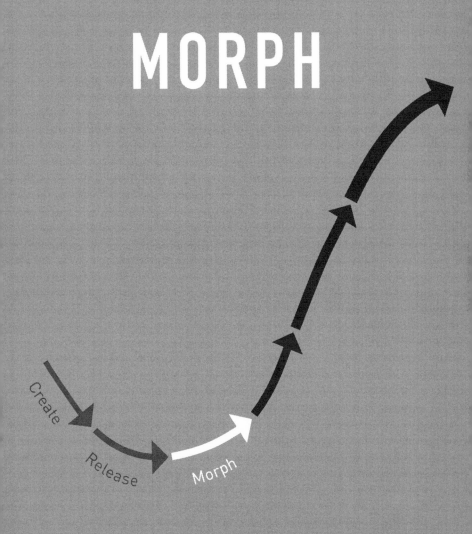

Create

Release

Morph

4

MORPH:
EMBRACE RADICAL CHANGE

The stereotypical start-up success story is quick and linear: The entrepreneur comes up with a genius idea, introduces it in the marketplace, and customers flock to it. The start-up goes from an unknown entity to a celebrated company and media darling, seemingly overnight. The general perception of a successful start-up path would be a straight, diagonal line, up and to the right.

Unfortunately, this stereotype is not reality, at least for most companies. Ninety percent of start-ups I have been involved with or observed need to make substantial, often drastic changes to their original plan, and those changes are usually difficult to make, both emotionally and practically. We refer to these changes, at this stage in the life of a start-up, as the *morph*. Most successful start-ups will have multiple morphs, because the first one or two may not work. Morphs are hard, and they will call upon all your available resources to pull them off. They will test your level of commitment. If you're only in this for your ego—if you see any criticism of your original idea as criticism of you—then you are going to struggle with this phase. If you possess a higher level of commitment—if you take the long view and want to build something substantial for yourself, your family, your employees, and your customers—then morphing will make sense to you.

Perseverance is a key to morphing. In fact, it's your greatest asset as an entrepreneur and is especially useful in this phase, since morphing is the proper response to failure. If you recognize and value making major project changes rather than viewing the process as negative, you can move through failure and morph with speed and alacrity. Remember that the only failure you should deeply fear is failure of the enterprise. Otherwise, accept smaller failures as necessary feedback that prepares you for the morphing process.

Intellectually and emotionally, the concept of morphing doesn't fit neatly into the straight-line success model. Rather, it suggests a rough and jagged road. Admitting that the great product idea with which you began the company, sold the investors on, and rallied the employees for is no longer viable is awkward, to say the least, and doesn't fit into the success story you imagined. You say to yourself, "Oh my God, I'm not Steve Jobs." No you're not, but don't fret, Steve Jobs wasn't Steve Jobs either when he started out. Prepare yourself for the Morph phase, which is full of stops and starts, and take all the feedback you acquired in the release phase and use it to re-create your product.

Morphing is not about making iterative, incremental changes—adding a feature, changing the packaging, or positioning the product differently through marketing materials. To morph effectively, major changes are required and they are often gut wrenching. Let's say you're a start-up Mexican restaurant; you're not morphing if you add fish tacos to your various taco selections. If not enough people are coming through the door, the fish tacos aren't going to save you, even if they're the greatest fish tacos ever made. This is where major changes should come into play. For instance, your Mexican restaurant discovers that customers are raving about your salsa. Your morph may involve packaging the salsa as a retail product and selling it in grocery stores and online. It may even require you to close the restaurant so you can focus your time, energy, and money on the packaged salsa.

Prepare to make major changes. To develop this change mindset, we need to examine the how and when of morphing.

PARAMETERS

The primary goal of the Morph phase is to obtain significant customer traction. Exactly what level of customer traction is significant will vary, but you'll know it based on the following signs: when customers are telling their friends about it, when it's being pulled from your hands rather than pushed into the customers' hands, and when its takes seemingly little effort to sell it. Until you get solidly into significant customer traction, you need to remain in the Morph phase, working to find and make a product that customers love.

The timing of the Morph phase varies from start-up to start-up, but in general, it will begin soon after you release the product. You know you're ready to morph based on customer response to your minimum viable product (MVP). Remember, the goal of the MVP is to prove your hypothesis. If you do prove it by gaining a meaningful amount of customer traction, then from that point, you will want to iterate, making incremental improvements based on customer feedback, building it out from minimally viable to a more full-featured product that eventually will gain a significant following, preferably from word of mouth.

However, this description represents the ideal flow, and most of the time, it's not that easy. Even after a few rounds of iterative improvements and tweaks, you may fail to gain meaningful customer traction. In that case, it's time to morph. A morph implies a fundamental change in product, market, or strategy— or all three. Some people refer to this as a pivot, though morph strikes me as a better term, since it connotes a more significant change: What you end up with may not look anything like what you started with.

Morphing signals your awareness that the initial MVP is not going to achieve what Marc Andreesen refers to as *product/market fit*, no matter how much you tweak it or how much marketing money you spend on it. Andreesen defines product/market fit as a good market with a product that can satisfy that market. You know you have reached it when you obtain meaningful customer traction.

To morph effectively, determine the direction you should take the product. As you'll recall in our discussion of the release phase, I emphasized paying attention to what customers deem right with the product rather than the things they find wrong; you can't fix your way to a great product. Here, focus even more intensely on customer feedback and combine that with your imagination and creativity to figure out your product direction. Tesla CEO Elon Musk put it best when he said, "The most important thing an entrepreneur can do is focus on making a great product or service. The only way to do so is by learning from the feedback loop of the market and constantly adjusting behavior."

To get to a great product quickly, ask yourself the following questions:

- What is working for your product?

- What are the customers talking and writing about?

- What about your product attracts customers?

- What do customers want more of?

- What aspect of the product appears to address a real need?

Once you figure out the direction, push hard toward it. Do more of what's right for your product and less of everything else. Brainstorm with your people. Write down every idea your team has, and then start winnowing down the list by eliminating any impractical (because of cost or for other reasons) ideas.

The litmus test of a successful morph is customer traction: Your customers are engaging with and loving the product, despite the obvious flaws that are always evident in any MVP. Of course, they still want improvements, but that is not stopping them from grabbing it off figurative shelves. More specifically, customers are buying with less effort than you expected; every graphed metric you possess is moving up and to the right; you've received praise from a variety of stakeholders—online reviews, industry observers, executives on your supply chain. And, best of all, everything you know tells you this positive trend will continue. Once you have this type of customer traction, you can stop morphing and go back to making smaller, iterative improvements.

Signs of a lack of customer traction, on the other hand, include the following: Customers are largely negative or indifferent about your product, traffic is not growing, repeat usage is limited, outside comments about your product are mediocre or worse, or your sales aren't closing. Everything feels like a push; it's a struggle to achieve even modest usage objectives. Without customer traction, you need to remain in the Morph phase, bringing out new versions, including their iterations, until one clicks.

You may need three to five morphs to get it right, and if you adopt a multiple-change mindset, you can morph quickly. Keep in mind that time is money, and you have limited funds, so the faster you can react, the more morphs you will be able to do. Think of these morphs as shots on goal. You keep shooting the puck at the goal until one goes in. The more shots you take, the more of a chance you have of scoring. Time is your enemy here: If you can't find product/market fit and get significant customer traction before the funds run dry, you will be in a difficult spot (see chapter 9 on failure).

WHAT A MORPH LOOKS LIKE

Even savvy businesspeople may assume that products will emerge full-blown, like Venus from a large seashell. They focus on the mature, highly successful product, rather than on all the changes that led to its final, successful form. As many times as I tell start-up founders that they will probably need to revolutionize their original product—and probably change it significantly more than once—they often cling to the notion that a tweak here or an evolution there will do.

Generally, it won't. Most times, you have to shift the product concept in major and, sometimes, unexpected ways. To drive this point home, let me tell you two stories.

First, you're probably aware of Adobe, the hugely successful desktop software publishing company. What you might not be aware of, though, is that when cofounders Charles Geschke and John Warnock left Xerox to create Adobe, they intended to make printers. At Xerox, they came up with highly innovative approaches to facilitating improved computer printing, and when they left, they believed that their business required them to create both computers and printers to capitalize on their ideas.

But then, Geschke and Warnock began talking to prospective customers, including Gordon Bell, at Digital Equipment, and Steve Jobs, at Apple. When they pitched Bell, he surprised them by explaining that he was happy with their computers and laser printers, but he was tremendously intrigued by the software capabilities of Adobe and how the software could facilitate the communication between computer and printer and increase the quality and capabilities of the printers.

Geschke and Warnock, though, were still focused on their original product concept and brushed aside Bell's suggestion. When they talked to Jobs and he basically told them the same thing (after trying unsuccessfully to buy their fledgling company), the idea sunk in. They needed to make a leap from the product idea of computers and printers to the product idea of software, which became known as Postscript. This was an enormous change—a morph of the highest order—and it was even harder, because they had raised money based on the hardware-oriented business plan. It can be rather awkward to go back to the investors that you have just fervently sold one business plan and explain that the original idea is not going to happen but you have another idea that you think has good chances. In my experience, however, investors are more understanding than expected. In this case Geschke and Warnock made it work, and Postscript went on to forever change the world of publishing. Turns out it was a rather large idea, as thirty years later, Adobe is still around as a public company and is worth over $40 billion.

Max Levchin and hedge fund manager Peter Thiel founded

PayPal in 1998, but in its original product form, it bore little resemblance to the web-based payment system most people are familiar with today. Back then, Levchin was a recent college graduate who specialized in cryptography software for handheld devices. His initial product, created for PalmPilots, involved providing security for users of these devices. The response was good, and Thiel helped fund the new company.

Handheld devices, however, never became the corporate standard as everyone had anticipated back in the late nineties. As a result, Levchin revamped the product, re-creating their PalmPilot security software for the consumer market. This was morph #1. At first, their product was designed to secure information, like credit card numbers and passwords. When the response to this product was lukewarm, Levchin re-created it again; the new product secured financial transactions. This was morph #2.

In this radically different form, the product was able to send money from one handheld device to another. In this way, if you owed a friend money, you could send it to him via handhelds and do so securely. Based on a demonstration of this technology, Levchin and Thiel were able to secure funding from venture capital firms, and they were in business.

But they weren't done with their morphing. As people began downloading their app for handheld devices, Levchin and Thiel also discovered that people were trying to use the company's website for their financial transactions. This surprised the founders, since they believed they had created a tremendously effective product for handhelds, and the website simply provided a demo for prospective customers.

Then, they were contacted by the online auction site eBay; eBay's representatives were interested in using their technology to secure financial transactions on their site. The eBay representatives were persistent, and Levchin and Thiel eventually recognized that the website market could dwarf the handheld device one.

In late 2000, they terminated their handheld device product and began focusing exclusively on providing secure financial exchanges for eBay users. This was morph #3, but they still weren't done. People had warned Levchin that fraud would be a problem, but he and his colleagues didn't realize how much of a problem until fraud began occurring regularly. As a result (and after much hard labor), they finally created a fraud-resistant version of PayPal. This was morph #4. You could also argue that it was a large iteration of morph #3 (at a certain point, measuring change is a matter of semantics). Having settled on the final version, the company had product/market fit: It had a product people loved in a quickly growing market.

This story's moral isn't only that you have to create a lot of versions of a product before it's successful, but that even brilliant entrepreneurs like Levchin and Thiel can enter the initial phases of a start-up with certain assumptions about their product and have their customers disabuse them of their assumptions. Being open and attentive to what the marketplace communicates is crucial during this phase. Levchin and Thiel were sufficiently receptive to what customers (and eBay) were telling them that they were able to jettison products that were tied directly to previous passions (software cryptography) and reconceptualize the company's product to produce PayPal.

HOW TO MORPH EFFECTIVELY

Discarding your original product in favor of one that gains customer traction may sound like a relatively simple exercise, but all sorts of obstacles can impede your progress. When I discussed the release phase, I noted that psychological as well as practical roadblocks can hinder a start-up's ability to traverse that phase successfully. The same holds true here. Founders of start-ups love their first products like they love their children; the Morph phase asks them to identify and accept the flaws in their offspring. Even more challenging, this action is analogous to giving up on the dream that their child will become a musical prodigy and allowing them to pursue an entirely different discipline.

The hyperbole of this metaphor isn't as much an exaggeration as you'd think. It's tough to morph, so to make it easier, here are some suggestions:

Prepare Yourself and Your Colleagues That a Morph Is Probably Coming

Think and talk about the inevitability of product change in advance. When you wrap your mind around the fact that you will probably need to leave your original product behind and create something quite different from what you envisioned, it's easier to accept when change becomes necessary. Help your investors understand that it's likely you will need to produce at least one major departure from the original so they aren't freaked out when you break the news in the morph phase.

Too often, morphing can feel like the precursor to enterprise failure to the uneducated and inexperienced. The first product didn't become a huge hit, so an air of doom and gloom settles on the start-up. In fact, failure of the firstborn is a natural part of the start-up process.

Think About Alternatives Even Before the Launch

They may not be the right alternatives—customer feedback will help make this determination—but forcing yourself to consider product options early on will help you develop a morph mindset. It may be that customer feedback will lead you to develop one of your early alternatives. Even if it doesn't, however, you will be more open to the morph process than if you had proceeded with one and only one product idea firmly fixed in your head.

Be Willing to Bend Over Backward to Obtain Customer Data

Talking to customers face-to-face and watching them is the best feedback of all, but you should also read comments online, personally take on customer service , conduct surveys, and make sure your product is priced low enough to be purchased by a sufficient number of customers. This will catalyze your major product changes, so go about collecting and analyzing the data with great energy and focus.

Be Creative

Innovation is the juice that will energize this phase. You're going to be absorbing a lot of information from customers, and then creatively mix this data with your original idea and come up with something new. Everyone has a different way of being creative. Some people love to brainstorm with colleagues. Others prefer to be off by themselves somewhere quiet to give their minds room to roam. Still, others have their own idiosyncratic process—they need to listen to music or they follow a brain-stimulation exercise—to catalyze their creativity. Give yourself permission to take all the information you obtain from customers and play with it. Don't place restrictions on what comes next. You want to try out all sorts of possibilities to find the one that best capitalizes on what customers are telling you.

Paul Graham, for instance, was a cofounder of Viaweb, a company started in 1998 that created software to help businesses design online stores. In its original form, Graham's software was focused on help-ing art galleries go online. Graham and his cofounder, Robert Morris, listened to their prospective art gallery customers tell them that they weren't interested in putting their artwork online. Instead of giving up or trying to convince their customers to embrace the future, they made a leap of imagination. What if they took the software they were writing for art galleries and made some changes so it would help all types of businesses create online stores? Then, they became even more creative. Initially, Viaweb was built for a desktop computer; the user would create a website and then upload it to a server. But then, Gra-ham and Morris took another creative leap: What if the user could control the software by clicking on web page links? As a result, they generated one of the first web-based applications as well as one of the first application service providers. Viaweb was eventually purchased by Yahoo and became the basis for its Yahoo! Store service.

Act quickly

On one hand, you don't want to flail around changing direction before your current release has had a chance to prove itself (or not), and it's OK to do an iteration or two on a particular morph, to give it a fair chance. But on the other hand, you want to get to the next morph as quickly as possible. So don't study the customer data like a scholar, spending weeks or months mulling it over. Remember, you may have to create two, three, or more new products, and the longer you wait, the less runway you will have to get it right. You want to have a tight cycle that goes from new release, to feedback, to perhaps an iteration or two, to another morph. Repeat this pro-cess until you get significant customer traction. Admittedly, needing to give a particular product more time or another round or two of iterations versus morphing to a new product idea is a paradox, and the decision of when to move on can be a tough one.

METAMORPHIC MISTAKES

These are big errors that are commonly made in this phase, all of which revolve around failing to make major changes. I cannot over-estimate the hold an original product idea has on an entrepreneur's mind. Terri Jannek, for instance, created a healthy-eating app that was designed to help people take their current diet and revise it based on the latest information about nutrition and healthy foods. When she pitched the idea, she received a highly favorable response from investors, including a well-known venture capital fund. Friends and family told Terri she was well on her way to wealth and fame because of her brilliant concept. With a tech background, Terri was able to design the app herself, and she released it using a well-known marketing firm that created a lot of buzz about the app.

But it didn't sell well. It turned out that while many people liked the concept of the app—of finding a simple, fast, inexpensive way to adjust their diets so they ate better—they didn't like the adjusted diets the app created. They may have been healthy, but they were unappetizing; not everyone wanted to eat kale chips and seaweed salad. Because the app wasn't tailored to individual tastes, it failed to sell.

But Terri was so convinced that it should sell that she couldn't let go of the original product concept. She had received so much positive response in the Create phase—and so much funding—that she convinced herself that sooner or later, the app would be successful. It wasn't, and the company folded.

Terri, like many entrepreneurs, made a Morph phase mistake. Let's start with her error and then look at other common mistakes:

Wishful Thinking

This is a close cousin of the Create phase mentality of *dreams unburdened by reality*. Dreams lead to wishful thinking, and this attitude can blind entrepreneurs to the points that customers are raising. They may have ample evidence they should morph, but they keep thinking that things will get better if they stay the course. Tesla CEO Elon Musk captured this mentality perfectly when he said, "I find it remarkable that I can explain the reality of a situation to people and still not change their point of view . . . Rather than learn from their experiences, they choose to engage in wishful thinking. Perhaps it's more comfortable than reality . . . [it's] the reason people adhere so strongly to wrong ideas . . ." (http://www.inc.com/leigh-buchanan /david-s-kidder-start-up-playbook-excerpts.html). The opposite of wishful thinking is intellectual honesty, and that is what will save you in this phase.

Belief You're One Tweak Away from Success

When start-up founders convince themselves they are on the cusp of a breakthrough, they often focus on the one small change they might make that will send them over the top. This is where feature creep occurs; they believe that if they just add one feature, customers will embrace their product. It's OK to do a quick tweak or iteration on a particular morph. A tweak, however, is not a morph. Don't make the mistake of spending time and money on a minor change when a full metamorphosis is called for.

Certainty That Better Marketing or More Money Will Save You

Instead of bringing out fresh iterations of the original product, these entrepreneurs convince themselves that spending more money on advertising or obtaining a fresh infusion of investment dollars will help get them over the hump. It's OK to spend a limited amount of money to obtain enough customers for critical feedback. But if the product isn't delighting customers, no amount of marketing or money will help in the long run. The right product will save you, so morphing is the only alternative.

Hubris

It's tremendously difficult for some entrepreneurs to accept that their original product idea didn't pan out. They've told friends and family about how great their idea is, impressed upon investors how it should make them a great deal of money, and lived with the product concept for months or years. As a result, it's difficult for them to abandon the idea and morph. It feels like failure. In fact, failure happens when entrepreneurs adhere blindly to their original product and fail to listen to customer feedback that the product needs to change. Pride in your work is good; excessive pride ensures that you'll cling to that product idea like a leaky life preserver and end up going down with it. Confidence in the collective abilities of yourself and your team is a good thing, but hubris is deadly.

THE MORPH PHASE CHECKLIST

In start-ups, as in life, people are resistant to change. If this is your first start-up, expect to encounter that resistance. Even after reading this chapter and raising your awareness of the mistakes made during Morph, you may struggle to move on from your original product idea and come up with something that is more than just a tweak or a new and improved version of the original. To increase the likelihood that you'll pursue the major changes that will help you morph successfully, take advantage of the following checklist:

- Are you designing a new product (from the original) based specifically on what customers are telling you? Is your feedback loop telling you what customers like about your product, what they want more of, and the particular product quality or feature that addresses a key customer need?

- Are you monitoring response to a morphed product through the lens of customer traction? Are you seeing praise from stakeholders and every financial indicator coming back positive? Or are you failing to generate traffic and receiving consistently negative comments?

- Have you taken early Morph phase steps to pave the way for major departures from the original concept? Have you talked about the possibility of other products besides the original with your colleagues and investors? Are you doing everything possible to obtain feedback from customers about your initial product; are you willing to be creative (i.e., think out of the box, take risks, entertain fresh thinking) to produce your new idea? Are you willing and able to move quickly to introduce your morphed product?

- Are you conscious of the mistakes that are commonly made during the Morph phase? Are you aware how wishful thinking, one-tweak-away mindset, marketing or money panacea, and hubris can prevent you from producing a successful second, third, or fourth product?

- Do you do more than give lip service to the idea of a morph? Do you accept that it's probably going to take a lot more than tweaks or new generations of the product to morph effectively? Are you willing to discard the original product in favor of something that may be far removed from what you first had in mind?

MODEL

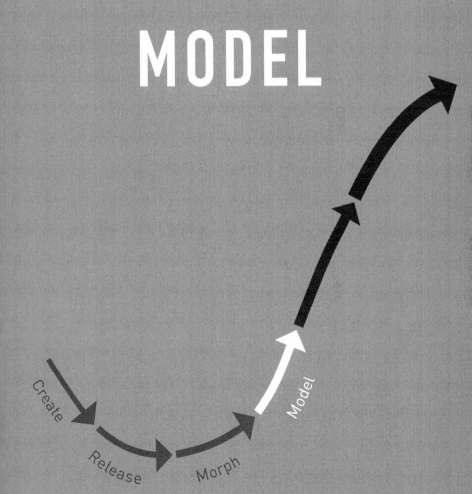

Create

Release

Morph

Model

5

BUSINESS MODEL:
NAIL IT BEFORE YOU SCALE IT

Having morphed your product to a stage where you've established a strong and growing customer base, your next job is to nail the business model, which determines how you make profits. The components of a business model involve three basic ingredients: (1) Produce the product (or provide the service). (2) Acquire a customer. (3) Generate revenue from that customer. You have a successful and profitable business model when #3 (revenue) is greater than #1 (cost of product) + #2 (sales and marketing). At its core, it really is that simple. The model needs to be built in a way that will help you be profitable at some specific point in the future—preferably sooner rather than later.

You may be thinking, *I've got that covered*, but your original preconceptions of what the model would be probably formed in the Create phase, and a lot has changed since then. As a result, your original ideas of how the business is going to make money may no longer fit what your business has become, and, if so, you need a new and improved model. In fact, I'd encourage you to chuck whatever ideas you had about monetizing and start with a blank slate. Look at the business as it exists today and ask yourself, *What is the best way to monetize this?* By taking a fresh look after you've found the right product & market, you can monetize your final product iteration most effectively.

To put yourself in this position, though, you've got to accept that it's normal for a business model to change from its original form; what you created when you first launched your start-up was only a placeholder. This isn't always easy for a start-up founder to accept. If you can adopt this perspective, however, you'll find it much easier to jettison the model you thought was a huge moneymaker but turned out to be ill suited to your evolving product and business.

When we started DealBase, we believed that organic search would fuel our growth but eventually discovered that we needed to purchase traffic through search engine marketing and other sources to build a decent business. The tradeoff—high cost of customer acquisition for increased customers and revenue—was essential. If we had stuck to our original organic concept, we never would have been able to scale effectively. Sam Shank saw the challenge quickly and didn't hesitate to make the switch. Talented start-up CEOs do that—when something clearly isn't working and isn't going to get you where you need to go, they move to plan B without hesitation. In fact, in this case, there wasn't even much of a discussion; Sam just did it. He hired a team that was incredibly adept at sourcing traffic and monetizing it. As a result, we were able to scale far beyond what we had originally expected.

ANOTHER HYPOTHESIS

The process of getting to the optimal business model is the same as getting to the right product. You start with a hypothesis, test it, listen to the feedback, and study the data, then you either iterate with incremental improvements or morph into another hypothesis. Rinse and repeat until you have a model that delivers solid profits. You don't need a model that produces profits immediately, but one that does so ultimately. If it can't fulfill this mission, then you are on a fool's errand, and scaling will only increase the losses. So getting the business model right is not optional; it's a requirement before moving to the next phase.

The good news is that it's generally easier to find the right business model than it is to get the product right because the number of foundational business models is more limited. In the digital media business, for instance, your primary revenue models are advertising and subscriptions (though variations exist with each of these approaches). If you're creating a software business, you'll opt for an enterprise sales model (a one-time fee plus maintenance) or a software as service (SAS) model (monthly fee). While endless permutations and new innovations exist, the fundamental building blocks tend to be the same.

Not many entrepreneurs get their hypothesis right from the get-go—where the money-making concept that they included in their business plan works in practice as well as in theory. For many of you, this hypothesis is going to change, and you need to be prepared to read the market so you know how it should change to make your company profitable.

As you may recall, when I discussed FlexJobs in the first chapter, the company provided listings of work-from-home jobs to employers and charged prospective employers for access to the service. Over time, however, we discovered our initial hypothesis was wrong—human resources departments were not willing to pay a substantial fee to find these remote workers. So we flipped the business model and tested another hypothesis. We gave the listings to employers for free and charged subscribers (the remote, work-at-home people looking for jobs) a nominal fee to gain access to these sometimes hard-to-find flex jobs. We gained enough in monthly subscription fees to become profitable and eventually grow into the market leader. Interestingly, a few years later, more mainstream employers began relying more heavily on remote employees. This allowed us to add an additional revenue stream; we circled back to the employers and offered them premium access to our established base of remote workers.

Some business models are better than others, and strong business models usually have some, or even all, of the following characteristics:

- High margins

- Low friction

- High leverage

- Network effects

- Repeatable

- Scalable

You'll want to possess a good grasp of each of these traits and try hard to incorporate them into the business model you're building.

HIGH MARGIN

I'm talking about high margins that are real, as opposed to ones that are figments of entrepreneurial imagination. I can't tell you how many business plans have been presented to me that project 60 percent net margins five years out. In fact, even the best businesses rarely ever reach 35 percent operating margins. Too often, entrepreneurs underestimate their costs and fail to realize that competition will require them to spend more on marketing than they expected and limit what they can charge. Despite what some politicians might say, the capitalist system in America is brutally competitive and extremely efficient at squeezing margins.

High margins can be defined in one of two ways—either on a percentage basis or via an absolute dollar amount. Software, web, and pharmaceutical companies are examples of the former—their cost of product and sales tend to be low relative to their selling price. Grocery stores, car dealers, and retailers like Amazon are examples of the latter—their cost of product and sales tend to be high. While companies like Amazon have received criticism for being low-margin businesses, they do OK in the end. If an average customer spends $3,000 annually and Amazon has 15 percent margins, they receive $450 from that customer. So while they may not make that much on an individual transaction, the cumulative total dollar volume can be high.

Capitalism entails a striking paradox. The goal of the system is to engender competition to encourage lower prices, but the goal of the competitors within the system is to avoid competition and thereby enjoy higher profits.

Competition kills margins, and in a perfectly competitive world, nobody makes any money. However, if you flip that statement upside down, you'll see that the corollary is also true: A lack of competition allows for high margins. The highest margins are typically enjoyed by companies that are unregulated monopolies, or nearly so. Monopolies are illegal, but if you look at the income statement of a company that has been accused of monopolistic behavior, such as Microsoft or Google, you'll find very high margins. So given that you want to seek high margins, you will want to think about what you can do to avoid competition. Competition may well be a good thing for consumers in a capitalist society, but as a start-up founder, think about where you reside on the competitive continuum in the Model phase—the closer you are to being dominant, the better your margins will be.

An example of a strong business that is hard to compete with is the Nebraska Furniture Mart, owned by Warren Buffett. Nebraska Furniture Mart carries the largest selection by far of any furniture store in Omaha. Because of their high sales volume, they also get the best discounts from manufacturers. Finally, because the items they sell are often heavy and bulky and also because people like to actually sit in a couch before they buy it, competition from online retailers is limited. These advantages form what Buffett refers to as a *moat* around the business, which makes it hard for other companies to compete with them.

Margins are also an indication of the strength of your business. Low margins are a warning sign and typically reflect that you are: (1) Failing to add enough value compared to what is otherwise available to the consumer, (2) in a tough market, or (3) operating your business inefficiently. A product that adds a lot of value will almost always be able to command high margins. A life-saving drug is a great example. When you are staring at the specter of the grim reaper, you'll spend a lot of money to delay getting to know him better. A drug that extends your life meaningfully is in the high-value-add category. On the other end of the spectrum, raw commodity businesses, like coal mining, have a limited amount of value that they can add. Customers can get a similar product from lots of places, and they will gravitate toward the lowest price. If your business has low margins, you may survive, but it's going to be a tough slog and may simply not be worth pursuing. Rather than slug it out while my competition is bludgeoning me, I prefer to keep working to improve the business model, and I suggest you do the same.

Array Health was started in 2008, and it provided health care exchanges for corporations that allowed them to offer a variety of health insurance options to their employees; they could choose from a variety of health care plans and from multiple health care providers. It also allowed the employers to control their costs because they would offer a fixed contribution, rather than commit to a defined benefit. The business model mandated that Array hire salespeople to sell their solution to corporations and then charge a monthly administration fee for each individual participant. However, after about eighteen months, progress was limited, and two problems became apparent: (1) It was both expensive and time-consuming to sell to the corporations, and (2) the Affordable Care Act passed, which meant that many smaller corporations would stop offering health care and push their employees toward government exchanges. So the Array CEO, Jonathan Rickert, decided to radically change the business model and morph to become a more software-focused company. Array would private label its exchange software to the large health insurance providers, who could then use Array's product to offer health insurance exchanges to their huge existing customer base. It turns out that it took about the same amount of effort to close deals to these large providers as it did to sell to the far smaller and fragmented corporate accounts. Importantly, the product itself didn't require much in the way of modification (which is quite often the case when you morph the business model). Before long, Rickert and his team had signed up some of the largest health care insurance providers in the country.

If you can build your brand, then you can also increase your margins. Admittedly, building a brand can be a long-term task, and a start-up founder generally isn't able to accomplish this task in the time available during this fourth phase. Still, everything moves more quickly in a digital universe, and some brands—such as Facebook or Twitter—have been created with astonishing speed. Creating a sustainable, durable brand is an objective that, if achieved, will help you maintain your ambitious margins. For instance, we bought a digital tech media company called GigaOM that had been in receivership for a few months. Once we began bringing it back to life, we were surprised that advertisers started coming to us with offers to runs ads at premium rates—even before we had an outbound sales force.

The power of the GigaOM brand continues to amaze us, and we are doing everything we can to grow and protect that asset. The same thing happened recently with the Twinkies brand. It went bankrupt but then was bought by private equity firms Apollo and Metropoulos, who deftly capitalized on its brand equity and brought it back in a big way. The older I get, the more respect I have for the power of brands.

LOW FRICTION

Friction is the bane of any business model, and you want to look for it and get rid of it wherever possible. Friction is anything that slows down or increases costs in producing or selling your product; it slows growth and shrinks margins because of increased costs. Friction comes in many forms—a lengthy sales process, for instance, or too many steps to produce the product. Friction can also include poor pricing, either too high or too low. Anything that makes a potential buyer slow the process down, avoid committing, or change direction can be friction. You should always be on the lookout for friction and how to reduce it.

Pierre Omidyar achieved low friction with eBay, the online marketplace. Because eBay only takes fees for transactions and never handles the actual merchandise, little friction exists in their business model. They don't have to find the goods, inventory them, finance them, merchandise them, interact with potential buyers, or pack and ship. As a result, they have low costs relative to revenue, producing excellent margins. eBay has one of the great business models of our time.

While creating a start-up with as little friction as eBay is a formidable task, every entrepreneur can reduce friction through simplification. As Steve Jobs said, "Simple can be harder than complex... but it's worth it in the end because once you get there, you can move mountains."

Think of simplification this way. Research shows that on any e-commerce site, a certain percentage of people will bail out at each point in the checkout process and especially when site visitors need to click to a new page. So a signup process that requires users to take five steps through five pages will have a lower conversion rate than a process that has only one or two steps or pages. While it may be easier from a technology and design standpoint to build a process with five steps, it creates friction for users—at each step, they ask themselves if they really want to do this. And a significant percentage may answer no. Taking friction out of the system can be hard and requires more work than building a sloppy high-friction system, but the reward is a better conversion rate. Better conversion rates mean you will gain more margin, which you can either retain or spend on marketing to grow your business faster. Entrepreneurs who address this issue tend to find it easier to generate revenue than other companies.

LEVERAGED

Business model leverage comes in many forms, but let's focus on two common ones. First, there's viral leverage—the ability to generate large numbers of users virally. This happens when your own user base spreads the marketing message and encourages others to use the product. While the term *viral* is thrown around loosely, true *virality* is achieved when each customer you obtain gains you more than one additional customer. If you reach this point, your viral coefficient is greater than one, and as long as you are not losing customers faster than you are gaining them, you're going to have some wonderful growth. A great example of a viral marketing phenomenon was the Ice Bucket Challenge, which raised money and awareness for ALS.

Though its origins are a bit difficult to determine, most sources suggest that individuals trying to raise money to fight ALS took to social media to publicize their fund-raising efforts, which were highlighted by taking a bucket of ice water and pouring it over their heads. In turn, they challenged others to follow suit, both with a watery immersion and a financial contribution. Soon thereafter, celebrities began participating, including *Today Show* host Matt Lauer in response to a challenge from pro golfer Greg Norman. Pro basketball player LeBron James and former president George W. Bush also participated. The mixture of social and traditional media publicity and celebrities helped catalyze the viral spread. Millions of views of ice bucket challenge videos took place on Facebook, and an equally large number of mentions occurred on Twitter. Most importantly, the ALS foundation received donations in excess of $100 million.

While this isn't a start-up example, it illustrates perfectly what a viral element can do when it's part of a business model. Creating buzz that travels from one person to the next in an astonishingly short period of time is the goal, and if an entrepreneur has a plan to create this buzz via an attention-getting, social media–friendly tactic, it's worth a shot. More to the point, if it works, it strengthens a model immeasurably. Virality is a great way to leverage your user base to spread your sales and marketing message and grow your business.

NETWORK EFFECT

The network effect describes the phenomena whereby the more people who use a product, the more valuable the product becomes. Business models that capitalize on this effect can create a substantial barrier to entry for competitors. Perhaps the most obvious example of the network effect is Facebook. When a small circle of friends were using the Facebook prototype at Harvard, it had limited appeal because most people were unable to find any friends on it that they knew. However, once it was adopted by 70 percent of the student body, users could find and interact with most of their peers. With each new user, the network became more valuable. The more valuable a network becomes, the easier it is for it to get more participants.

eBay also has a strong network effect, in that the more variety of goods it has available, the more useful the service is to potential buyers. The increasing number of buyers that the site attracts makes it more useful for sellers, who in turn list more goods, resulting in more variety. This positive spiral represents a powerful network effect.

Size matters when it comes to network effects, and there tends to be only one winner in that type of category. Here's how I had my epiphany about this effect. After graduating from college, I bought a seat on the New York Futures Exchange (NYFE) to trade stock index futures. The NYFE competed with Chicago's S&P pit, but the latter had about 40 percent more trading volume, resulting in better liquidity and execution prices. Because of this, the S&P pit got the majority of the orders and those orders, in turn, created a better product (better execution prices and faster order fills). It soon dawned on me that volume breeds volume in that the more volume the S&P got, the more volume it attracted. I could see the delta widening each week. So despite the fact that the NYFE was backed by the venerable New York Stock Exchange, the NYFE was destined to lose the race to the Chicago S&P pit. The NYFE was eventually merged into another exchange, and the S&P pit remains the dominant stock index futures trading pit thirty years later.

One of the companies I'm currently investing in, BounceChat, is an app that offers local social sharing. It allows users to share messages and images based on distance from their location, and originally, the company wanted to market it for events such as concerts. The founder, Gordon Free, was a professional DJ and attended many music events. He wanted a product that would allow everyone present to share. Unfortunately, the window for connections at a concert was brief—the duration of the event—and afterward, there lacked a compelling reason to continue to use it because people traveled out of range. Eventually, we realized that if we targeted small—if we tried to generate users within a confined geographical area like a high school or college—we might gain critical mass one school at a time and eventually achieve a network effect. You can see how this is a real morph, since connecting kids at a small high school is quite a bit different from what Gordon had in mind originally. This highlights the kind of dexterity and flexibility that you need when you are trying to figure out the model. Having the network effect as part of its business model will be a big help for BounceChat.

REPEATABLE

Your model isn't fully baked until you can show that it is repeatable. Some start-ups begin with a bang and then fizzle out. They may attract customers initially because they offer one-time incentives or because they have good relationships and convince people to give their product a try or because of the sheer novelty of what they offer—or, in some instances, start-ups give their products away to encourage usage. Whatever the reason, gaining these initial customers doesn't guarantee anything. It's only when you demonstrate the ability to make sales repeatedly that you have a model you can take to the next phase.

The litmus test for repeatable varies, but for example, if you are a business-to-business (B2B) operation, you should be able to make multiple sales to a variety of companies—especially companies where you have had no previous contact (so you're not trading on past favors). Ideally, you have hired a successful salesperson, proving that you possess a sound product and strategy that isn't dependent on your previous relationships or selling ability. In our BounceChat example, nailing one high school is a good start, but we won't know we have a repeatable model until we nail three or four, or better yet, five or ten. Repeatable is an essential quality if you hope to scale your product.

SCALABLE

Ultimately, if you want to build a substantial business, you will need a model that is scalable. A model that scales is one where you can invest money and grow substantially without hurting the product (or service) and without hurting the business model. Ideally, you are looking for a business that gets *better* as you scale it. This happens when you gain competitive advantages as you grow.

Walmart is a company that has many scale advantages, beginning with the fact that it is so large and has so many customers that suppliers are almost required to sell through them. Walmart leverages this into negotiating rock bottom prices from suppliers, and this in turn allows them to beat the competition on price and thereby grow their customer base. There are other related economies of scale that Walmart enjoys, such as distribution, advertising, and new store construction. When you add them all up, it makes Walmart hard to compete with. You could see, by contrast, that a consulting business would be harder to scale. You may be a great consultant, but the next few people you hire could very well not be as good as you are, and clients will notice the difference. So as you try to scale, the service may suffer.

Generally, it's more difficult, more capital intensive, and more time consuming to scale a business-to-business model than a consumer one. The former requires a concentrated sales effort and a longer time frame to evaluate and decide about a product. A consumer business, on the other hand, has the advantage of a potentially greater number of customers, lower price points, and the ability to make quick buying decisions on their own.

Before moving to the next phase, Scale, you want to think about how you can ensure that your model can be scaled and what the right, realistic, and appropriate growth rate might be.

THE MODEL PHASE CHECKLIST

Throw out the business model that you brought to the start-up, or at least be willing to reassess it and determine if it's viable. If you do a quick before-and-after analysis—before Morph and after—you'll probably identify changes that have rendered your earlier model obsolete. It's time to trade in for a new one, or at the very least a vastly improved one, and the following questions will help you do so:

- In what significant ways has your product changed? How do these changes affect your original idea about how the business will make money? Do these changes suggest a new hypothesis about how your start-up will and should produce revenue?

- Have you made an objective, accurate assessment of your business's margins (or are you insisting that you can generate net margins above 50 percent in a matter of months or years)? Have you determined if your best margin approach is on a percentage or absolute dollar basis?

- Are you committed to building your brand in order to maintain good margins? Are you also focused on finding a way to dominate competitors to achieve the same goal?

- Do you have a leverage method that's part of your model designed to generate a large number of customers virally? Do you also have a process in place that will minimize friction?

- Does your model attempt to create a network effect? Are you focusing on creating that effect among a relatively small number of people and using that effort as a basis for widening the effect?

- Is your model repeatable? Will you be able to create repeat sales among a sizable customer segment using your current approach?

- Is your model scalable? Can you expand your customer base virally, globally, and in other ways using your existing processes and methods?

SCALE

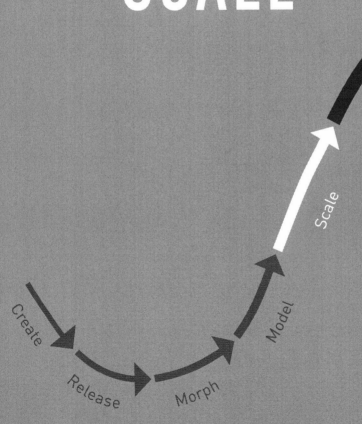

Create

Release

Morph

Model

Scale

6

SCALE: GO BIG WITH PEOPLE, PROCESS, AND MONEY

Once you've gained customer traction and nailed the business model—*and only when those steps are accomplished*—you're ready to take the next step. This point of emphasis is to remind you that you shouldn't scale prematurely—a common failing of many start-ups. I'll talk about this failing a bit later, but for now, make sure you don't even think about scaling until you have a product that a sizable number of customers love *and* you have nailed the business model.

If you've achieved this goal, then you're ready to scale, and there are three primary ingredients to scale effectively: people, processes, and money. You need more and better in all three categories. As you grow the business, you can no longer rely on free-wheeling generalists—I call them cowboys—who helped launch the business. It's time to find specialists who are experts in various functional areas; to improve your financial, human resources, technology, and other processes so they fit with the larger, broader company you're becoming; and to make or raise the money that a growing enterprise requires.

GET THE TIMING RIGHT

Shakespeare said "ripeness is all," and though he probably wasn't referring to start-ups, his observation is particularly relevant in the Scale phase. Start to scale only when the company and product is at the perfect point of ripeness. You have a relatively small window of time in which to scale the company, so you need to know precisely when to do so.

Scaling at its fundamental level involves doing massively more of everything. When you get bigger, a lot of pressure is exerted on every part of your start-up, and if you scale at the wrong time, that pressure can destroy the company. Think of a race car with slightly faulty parts; these defects may not matter at slow speeds, but at high speeds, things are going to break, and it's going to end in an ugly mess. If you have a gas leak, if the pistons don't quite fit, if the bolts aren't tightened, or if the wheels are not on properly, you're likely to crash when you get to high speeds. Similarly, if you *scale before you nail* the business model, you'll have a larger faulty business model, which means you'll lose lots of cash instead of a little, and that's not going to end well.

At the same time, if you wait too long, you will cede opportunities to your competitors. By the time you are ready to scale, it's a good bet that all of your credible competitors have heard about you. They have probably studied you, and many are concocting competitive products—if they don't already have them. So it's not a good time to dillydally. If you procrastinate, even though you have a great product and business model, then you will risk losing your chance to capitalize on all the potential revenue because you've allowed other, bigger companies to capture your market before you've grown into it.

Eventually, you'll need to figure out the *speed* at which you will scale. I wish I could give you a one-size-fits-all answer, but I have found that every business has a different optimal growth rate. You're in the best position to identify the natural rate of growth for your start-up, and you can do so by feel. Does it feel like you're missing excellent opportunities because you're refusing to grow even though you have customers in love with your product? Or do you feel frustrated and have less money on hand because you're trying to get big before you have the traction you require?

CHANGES: PEOPLE, MONEY, AND PROCESSES

When you are ready to scale, prepare your company to operate as a much larger entity. It's not simply that you need more employees; you need different types of employees. You also require additional capital and will need to alter the processes that surround the product—everything from financial to human resources to distribution.

That's a lot to do, so to help you get started, let's examine each of the three categories where big changes are required:

People

The individual employees who have been tremendously valuable up to this point (including, possibly, yourself) may become liabilities if they can't adjust to the rapidly growing company. Most start-ups thrive in the early phases because of their independent thinkers who question and test constantly. They are cowboys in the best sense of that term—rugged individualists who are comfortable on the product frontier. They also tend to be generalists because, as a tiny start-up team, each person usually needs to perform a wide variety of tasks.

As you get bigger, though, you require specialists who are experts in key functions such as product management, engineering, and finance. No longer do you want your generalists wandering into areas that are now properly covered by specialists. The specialists are trained professionals and they will resent the shoot-from-the-hip cowboys who will question everything, even though, typically, the cowboys will have less-formal training and expertise in that particular function.

Generalists and cowboys are part of a bygone era for your company, and if these terms describe your founding team, prepare for some difficult discussions. You and your inner circle need to decide on your individual areas of expertise and then focus exclusively on them. You will need to relinquish control in functional areas where you're not a seasoned expert. Be ready for a challenge, since you built the company without these clear job boundaries, and you're accustomed to everyone weighing in on everything. The kumbaya sessions in which everyone collectively makes a decision that everyone feels good about are over. People are going to complain and tell you that you're destroying what made the company great, that you're taking the fun out of work, that you're trying to be like a Fortune 500 corporation. The key, of course, is to preserve the essence of what has made the company successful so far, focus on the mission, keep it fun, and try to avoid becoming complacent, slow, and unimaginative.

In reality, you're trying to survive and thrive in a different form, and that means identifying and defining everyone's roles. If the existing employees can grow and adapt by focusing exclusively on a specific functional area they love, that is ideal. But doing so can be tough personally, and some will not be able to make the transition. If that's the case, they don't belong in the scaling company and are likely to be a problem. Invariably, some of your people will leave, and some you may have to part ways with. If you can hire new people who fit what is needed for the Scale phase, you are that much closer to Harvest. But among the three requirements for the Scale phase—people, money, and processes—getting the right people is the toughest task you face.

You are looking for people who have experience working for larger companies—often much larger companies. Avoid bringing in people who might be a good fit now but will be a poor fit a couple of years from now. You don't want to rehire every time your company takes another growth step. As you contemplate your candidates, prepare to *overhire*, in the sense that you want people who can do more than the current required role. Get in front of the growth instead of trying to keep up. As Wayne Gretzky once said, "I skate to where the puck is going to be, not where it has been." Target individuals who can help you as you become big and, then later, as you become bigger.

Scaling is expensive for several reasons. Until this point, experience has not been a requirement, and in fact, as we have seen, lack of experience and naïveté can be beneficial. In the scaling phase, however, naïveté can kill you. You want to bring on talent that has significant experience. You want to hire folks who have been there, done that. These individuals are expensive because of their experience and expertise; they have often attended impressive schools, earned graduate degrees, and have demonstrated competence in areas critical to your growing company.

Be aware, too, that you or your colleagues may feel threatened by managers and senior leaders who possess more experience or a higher specialized skill level than you do. You may also be so loyal to your current employees that you rationalize that they'll be able to grow with the company, but many will struggle to do so. Be conscious that you're going to resist bringing in new people for these reasons, and make a concerted effort to overcome this resistance. If you don't hire ahead of the curve, you're going to be in trouble, especially when you scale.

If you scale effectively, you're going to keep expanding and needing people who can show you the ropes during escalating stages of growth.

Money

It's tough to scale on the cheap. Don't be naive about how much capital it requires to expand your operation. Paying the experienced and highly skilled individuals we just discussed requires a bigger personnel budget than in a nonscaled company, and that's only one of the costs you'll incur as you scale. You can't attract talent without offering salaries commensurate with that talent; and you can't scale successfully if you don't have that talent in place. Scaling users also usually requires getting the word out about your product in a big way, and that kind of marketing and sales effort is expensive. Also expensive is rolling out the distribution, service, and support infrastructure to support the increased customer base.

Ideally, you'll generate cash flow based on your sales. If you've gained customer traction and people love your product, the odds are that your revenues will increase significantly. Whether it's significant enough for your expansion needs, though, is another question. Therefore, consider going to venture capital (VC) firms to raise additional funds. While I discouraged most of you from pursuing the VC route in the Create phase, here it may be a good option, because VCs love to invest large sums of money in companies that have a terrific product, strong customer traction, an established business model, and a desire to get big.

VCs offer start-ups a host of advantages from a scale perspective. Beyond the money, of which they often have a considerable amount to invest, they also tend to be great at scaling. It's their specialty, and they have watched and helped a lot of companies do it. They generally have great Rolodexes and can get you access to top professionals, such as lawyers and recruiters, as well as talented employees. Because they have seen so many companies scale, both with good execution and bad, they're familiar with what needs to happen, and they can provide excellent advice when needed. If you are going to require additional funding rounds, they are particularly adept at helping you get it during this phase. In fact, I have often been shocked at how good they are at financing. If I am on a board of a VC-backed company that is in the Scale phase and the discussion turns to financing, I usually try to keep my mouth shut (which is really hard). They can also possess the contacts (i.e., investment bankers) and the knowledge to help you navigate the Harvest phase.

Processes

Aside from meeting people and financial requirements, scaling requires process. If you are a software company, you used to be able to do a release the moment you deemed it better than the current live release. But at that time, you probably didn't have many customers, so if you broke something, it was relatively easy to remedy, and the cost was little, if anything. But when you are scaling and acquiring large amounts of customers, you will pay a heavy price for putting out a faulty release. Customers will panic, your customer service employees will be overwhelmed, the media will be alerted, and suppliers and partners will get nervous. In other words, all hell will break loose. It will cost you real money to fix, not to mention your staff being completely diverted from their normal duties and operating in a tense, frenzied, fire-drill mode. You simply can't make these types of mistakes anymore, and the way you avoid them is by having a rigorous testing and release process in place. Yes, this will slow down a new release somewhat, but at this point, losing a bit of speed is more than a fair tradeoff for getting the release right. There will be all sorts of other processes that you will want to put in place. Your accounting may need far more than QuickBooks. You may need a hiring policy, a vacation policy, an expense-approval policy, a dress code, a 401(k) plan, health plan, etc. You may need to implement regularly scheduled staff meetings to ensure communication that previously happened serendipitously at the water cooler. These processes and systems facilitate scaling at a healthy rate without driving everyone crazy.

You know that it's time to implement a process when you experience repeated fire drills around the same issue. Fire drills are time consuming, expensive, and frustrating for all involved. You don't want to lose the flexibility and dexterity to move quickly and respond to real situations or opportunities. At the same time, it's not healthy or advisable to move as suddenly and as sharply as you once did. Processes protect the brand, the revenue, and the people by keeping fire drills to a minimum.

SPREAD THE WORD

Sales and marketing are usually the key engines to growth in the Scale phase. This isn't the time to be secretive or coy: It is the time to sell the hell out of your product. Prior to Scale, marketing wasn't a priority; you only needed to obtain a sufficient number of customers in order to set up a good feedback loop. But once you have customer traction and a strong business model in place, you want and need customers—lots of them.

Use whatever marketing tactics have worked to get you where you are, and ramp up whichever ones can scale. Don't limit yourself to any one approach, and be aggressive about testing a variety of new channels. Consider ways to create a social media buzz, even if you favor traditional advertising methods; using blogs to get the word out is great, but it may be that a story in a well-respected, established print publication might generate momentum for your product. Look to create synergies by using a variety of marketing tools, including grassroots efforts such as creating word-of-mouth talk about your product.

There is an old management adage: You can't manage what you can't measure. If you can't measure what you're doing, you're guessing, and, especially at this stage, basing your marketing strategy on guesses doesn't scale. Be *very* rigorous about tracking effectiveness of all of the various marketing channels. Again, intellectual honesty is your friend because there are endless ways to fudge the numbers in marketing. Ideally, you want marketing strategies that scale—things that you can do in a big way if the numbers work.

Mistake #1: Accepting Lowball Offers

As you spread the word, other companies will notice you've got a terrific product and a loyal and growing customer base. Not only will your potential customers take note of this, but those who are either direct or tangential competitors will as well. Depend on it. It becomes harder for those competitors to dismiss you out of hand. They see your advertisements, read your press clippings, and hear their own customers (and maybe their employees) talking about you. The CEO will start receiving emails from the product managers. Their sales teams will start losing sales to you. In short, you become a thorn in their side.

The smart and alert competitors will investigate your company and product. In many cases, they will begin an internal effort to directly compete, often under the code name of: *(Insert your product name)-Killer.* While these efforts may cause you some heartache, and a little paranoia can be healthy, you should also know that they rarely succeed—at least initially. The enlightened competitor CEOs will ask themselves whether your product really is better or if it can be sold alongside their product into their already developed channel. If the answer is yes, then soon, you will receive a nonthreatening, semifriendly email or call indicating their interest. While they may be communicating for all sorts of reasons, it's most likely that they would like to take you out as a competitor and do so at the cheapest possible price. They realize that the sooner they buy you, the less expensive it will be.

It's tough to think clearly when you receive that buyout offer. I know when somebody asks to buy your company, it's a bit like being asked to the prom. How nice, somebody actually *appreciates* me, somebody realizes I'm a *genius* and that we have an *amazing* product or company or team or vision or whatever! And of course, you instantly fantasize that you are going to be rich. Soon, you're imagining the new house, private school for the kids, a new Tesla, and a ski vacation in Gstaad, Switzerland. And given all you have been through to reach this point, you're thinking that it's all going to pay off in one quick deal . . . *Alleluia!*

Your suitor starts by flattering you, insisting that you're indeed a genius. Then the next moment, he's not-so-subtly threatening to create their own product and do it themselves. They will crush you if you don't capitulate or sell. Your mood swings wildly from dreaming of that new Tesla or second home to the still-fresh recall of near-death experiences. You're a borderline manic as you swing from *I'm going to be rich* to *I could hit the wall and end up in a yard sale*. Money aside, you see the possibility that your mission and vision will finally be realized.

I hate to be a killjoy, but these buyout offers aren't what they seem to be. Let me make a case for why, in most cases, you should view them as a mistake waiting to happen. In the scaling phase, value creation gets going in earnest. What the J Curve graphically points out is that there is not that much value creation during the first few phases. In fact, quite often, there is value destruction—you are worth less than when you started. That's fine and entirely natural, but once you hit the scaling phase, you have a real business, one that is growing in size and value every day. You've worked your fanny off to get to the place where you can now create real value, for the world and for shareholders, and my advice is: Don't throw it away.

Yes, you may be worth two or three times as much as you were at the start-up's inception, but if two or five years have passed, then you're not going to be giving much of a return to yourself or your investors given the risk you have all taken. Plus, the money you receive from selling your business isn't as much as it might seem. After the government takes almost half of it and you buy that Tesla and take that ski vacation to Gstaad and buy your significant other various trinkets that he or she deserves after sticking with you during the tough, crazy years when you acted like a freak, you will soon be looking for another gig. But you will be right back at the beginning of the J Curve and looking at another long slog just to get where you already were. Ouch. At this stage, it's rare for a buyout offer to be a game changer for your lifestyle.

By contrast, if you make it through this phase and into the Harvest stage, the offers are quite often game changers, and they can set you up for life, if that is what you are indeed seeking. Even if you don't want to retire in the Harvest stage (most never do), you'll at least have enough marbles to play more start-up games.

Larger companies that make you an offer when you're beginning to scale aren't stupid. They realize you're probably approaching burnout and running low on funds; they want to take advantage of your desire to reap at least some reward from all your hard work. So they pounce. Don't expect them to over-pay because you're a company with great potential or because you're a brilliant leader; it's rare to get a strategic premium at this stage. They often have to answer to their board and shareholders, so they will pay as little as they can get away with. I've often heard the maxim that *you can't go broke taking a profit*, which I believe is deeply flawed. I prefer the maxim *you can't get rich selling*. The only way you can become a billion-dollar company is to turn down the offer for $5 million and $20 million and $100 million and $500 million along the way. Because if you really have something, it's a certainty you will get offers.

If I haven't dissuaded you yet from taking an early buyout offer, perhaps the huge expense associated with even considering such an offer will do the trick. Once word gets out that you're considering a sale—and word always gets out—the excitement, fear, and uncertainty surrounding the sale will kill whatever momentum the company has. I've seen businesses come to a full stop when word of an acquisition comes out. Suddenly, you are likely to find your product-release dates and your quarterly sales numbers in jeopardy. If that is not painful enough, suddenly everyone wants to have a discussion about equity, because now, the company is actually worth something. Equity discussions are often fraught with peril—people can easily get bent out of shape if they feel they're not going to get their fair share. And by the way, most people don't feel they have a fair share, in part because it's a highly subjective discernment. This is best addressed early in a company's life cycle with a well-defined process for providing options.

Another substantial problem, especially if the buyout offer is from a current or future competitor, is that you may find yourself in an awkward bind regarding the information required by the other side for due diligence. In order to advance the acquisition discussions, you will need to begin providing loads of information, and a lot of that information will be sensitive competitive data that can and will be used against you. The potential acquirer has asymmetric returns from this endeavor. They risk little other than their time, and they have a huge upside, either because the acquisition actually goes through or because they gain a trove of competitive information.

Finally, if you intend to sell the company, you really need to seek another bidder. In doing so, you have to make your intentions public, and invariably, your customers will learn that you're for sale. The effect will be to freeze the sales pipeline as customers wait to see how everything will shake out—only then will they make the decision about who will be their supplier.

Did I mention I hate early buyouts? I should, however, acknowledge that three situations exist where it makes sense to take an offer in this phase:

1. The management team or board is split on strategic direction, and there doesn't appear to be a way to resolve the conflict.

2. You know that you lack the passion and drive to make it through the Scale phase and can't find a replacement for yourself.

3. The acquiring company can do a better job than you can with running your company, potentially creating more value than you could.

I sold the first company I started, Inmark Development, for this last reason. My cofounders, Cliff Ribaudo, Mark Anders, and Peter Handsman, and I were selling quote display and technical analysis tools to financial services vendors such as Quotron and Dow Jones. At the time, numerous operating systems existed, but our engineers found a way for our development tools to create software that would work on all systems. We were doing well. We moved to Silicon Valley and became a player in the software tools market. But then I realized that, as CEO, I was not in a position to take the company any further than it was. Large platform vendors such as Microsoft and Sun were giving away tools in order to obtain platform market share, and our competitors were in a much better position than we were to capitalize on the market. So when we got an indication of interest from Rogue Wave Software in Corvallis, Oregon, we pursued it. Soon after meeting the CEO, Tom Keffer (who held a PhD), I realized he was much smarter than I was about the tools market. I also quickly gained a lot of respect for his COO, Dan Whittaker. There was little doubt in my mind that they would do a better job with our assets than I would. Additionally, if we merged, the resulting company would have the scale to compete in the field and possibly to go public. I'm glad we moved forward, as Tom and Dan did a great job, and the resulting company was able to scale in a way that we never would have been able to do alone. I transitioned to being on the board, which was a great experience, and we ended up doing an initial public offering (IPO) less than a year later. So while I tend to be wary of most early buyouts, this one was different because it produced a merger which leveraged our assets and led to a huge win for everyone.

Mistake #2: Scaling Prematurely

I've listed this as the second mistake, but it's probably the most pernicious. I discussed the importance of timing earlier in the chapter, but you need to understand why this is such a dangerous trap for start-ups in order to avoid this mistake. Nothing kills a start-up faster than a founder who scales based on hopes and dreams rather than a solid base of product/market fit and a great business model. In the venture capital community, premature scaling is a leading cause of start-up death. Big money can be lost when a company, often flush with cash, prematurely hits the gas pedal. In many instances, part of the problem is that they possess too much money, which can paper over problems with the product or model. An overabundance of funds also encourages you to scale, whether you are ready or not. The investors will wonder if you hesitate, and the money will be burning a hole in your pocket.

Entrepreneurs, like most people, tend to spend whatever money they have, and if they have an infusion of cash (i.e. from venture capital), they burn through it fast. They don't pause to think about whether they have all their ducks lined up in a row—or all their customers lined up and loving their product. All they know is that they have someone—often a venture capital firm—that believes they are on the verge of greatness and is willing to give them a large sum of money to get over the top. Perhaps it's natural to respond in this way to too much money, but here's a cautionary tale that may help you think twice before making this mistake.

Founded in 2007, GigaOM became a much-revered tech media start-up. Providing insightful stories about the tech business as well as holding well-attended and well respected conferences, GigaOM was a hot company that attracted venture capital money. Their blog and event product mix was effective, but like many high-profile online media companies, they struggled with how to generate cash. Nonetheless, they had a sterling reputation for high-quality writing about the tech industry and, as a result, eventually received $20 million in venture capital money.

As I noted earlier, venture capital firms need for a few of the companies in their portfolio to become massive. So VCs tend to get riveted on scaling. Using its surplus of VC money, GigaOM decide to scale by creating and growing a research division. It's easy to see why this strategy appealed to GigaOM—it offered the opportunity to make a great deal of money through research subscriptions, and they could capitalize on their reputation for knowledge and superior critical analysis of the tech sector. On top of that, they could use some of their existing employees to help create new, saleable products in the form of longer (than the site's blogs) think pieces.

In 2009, they launched their research division, offering their services at a low $79 per year subscription price. The thinking was that if they could create a large-volume response, they would have a solid base on which to expand their business. At the same time, however, creating this research operation was expensive. They needed to hire research professionals, salespeople, and marketing professionals for the new division as well as increase other overhead expenses (for instance, more office space for the additional staff).

Five years later, they went out of business. It wasn't that their research business was a bad business—it did generate a significant amount of additional revenue. But GigaOM, despite its success on the editorial side, hadn't nailed their overall business model and hadn't created a large and loyal group of research customers before they scaled. It's possible that if they had taken the research business slower and gradually built a large group of customers who loved their research services, they might have survived and thrived. But the pressure was on to get big in order to provide a large return on their substantial VC funding, and the premature scaling ultimately killed the business. We ended up buying GigaOM through one of our companies that we helped incubate called Knowingly, run by the talented Byron Reese. In order to make it work, our general plan is to rewind the tape and go back to the Model phase, properly figure out the business model, and then resume scaling.

How do you know when you're scaling prematurely? Test whether you've nailed the business model by asking the following question: If you stopped expanding today, would your business be profitable within three months? If your answer is no, you should ask what you would need to do to make it profitable and cash-flow positive. On the other hand, if you are quite sure you would be profitable if you stopped expanding, then you have the business model nailed enough to move definitively into Scale mode. I understand that some will say, "Gee, I can't get profitable within three months but I'm sure I can do it within eight." My response is that it's too hard to see accurately beyond three months, so beware that you may be fooling yourself. Others may say that they can't get to profitability unless they get to a certain scale. If this is indeed the case, you are on a perilous path, and my recommendation is to focus on a narrower market where you can prove the model.

ROLE AND CULTURAL CHALLENGES

Scaling presents founders and their teams with a hurdle that doesn't exist in the other phases. Here, your roles are going to change. Let's say your start-up has two founders, Dave and Bill. They've made it through the long, cold winter—the downward slope of the J Curve—and have finally achieved product/market fit, strong customer traction, and a fully baked business model. Bill is an engineer by training and naturally assumed control of all of the start-up's engineering-related decisions. But in the beginning, he was involved in other areas by necessity—no one else had sufficient expertise in a number of functional disciplines. As a result, Bill was heavily involved in marketing, sales, and customer support and prided himself on his ability to become proficient in these areas. When the company scaled, though, Dave and Bill agreed they needed to bring in functional experts to handle the more complex and sophisticated issues that arose in a much larger organization.

As they talked about the need to bring in a marketing VP, Bill agreed this was necessary, but Dave worried that Bill would interfere constantly in the new marketing executive's decision making. In order for the organization to scale, Bill needed to get out of the way of the new marketing guy, and, at first, he struggled to do so. He was constantly second-guessing the new person's decisions, and his refrain, "You know, that's not how we handle marketing in this company," irritated the new marketing executive.

Dave realized he had to have an uncomfortable conversation with his partner. He tried to spin the talk in a positive way. He told Bill that the company needed him to focus exclusively on his area of specialization, and they needed him to use his engineering expertise because that function was growing rapidly. Eventually, Dave told Bill that he needed to adapt or leave; he was concerned that they were going to lose the talented marketing executive if Bill didn't resolve to stay out of his way. It was an awkward, unpleasant conversation, but fortunately, it helped Bill understand the seriousness of the problem, and he eventually adapted to his new, specialized role.

From a cultural standpoint, prepare yourself for the organizational environment to change. I'd write that you should prepare for cultural change, but many of you may roll your eyes at that term, saying to yourself, "I can't believe that we are talking about corporate culture." After all, you became an entrepreneur and launched a start-up because you wanted to do your own thing. Perhaps in the past you worked for a large organization and hated the culture—the politics, the endless meetings, the hierarchical way of relating to other employees.

As you become a larger company, however, you're going to need policies and processes. Without any sort of rules or procedures, it's too difficult to run a large and growing company effectively. In the initial phases of the start-up, it's quite possible that everything was loosey-goosey and you made major decisions by the seat of your pants, that transparency and participative decision making were the norms. Anyone could say anything about anything.

But with scaling comes specialization, and the nature of increasingly large, specialized functions means that nobody knows everything; that for the company to operate efficiently, processes need to coordinate the efforts of various specialists and make sure the people who are in the best position to decide are the ones who do decide. Even the loosest, largest Silicon Valley companies require some form of structure and some cultural norms.

So reconcile yourself to this necessity, decide what type of culture you want to have, and make sure it is tied into the company mission. As the CEO or senior member of management, you should be repeating and reinforcing the company mission and culture at every opportunity. As the company grows, this is what will keep the people together and focused. It doesn't have to be a traditional, top-down, controlling culture. Just because you're getting bigger doesn't mean you have to become a Fortune 100 corporate clone. But you do have to think and talk about how you're going to deal with everything from decision making to meetings to office communication to team structures. In this way, you can help evolve the culture into something that fits your vision for the company, even as it grows into something that looks nothing like the start-up from phase 1.

(NOT) GOING GLOBAL

The press and the intelligentsia continually talk about the fact that we live in a global economy. As soon as you start to have some modicum of success, you may feel the pressure to go global. There are several substantial problems with this. The first is that virtually everyone underestimates the frictional costs of selling a product in another country: the distribution is expensive, the legal issues complex, the hiring practices challenging and expensive, and the market is different, as is the culture. In short, it's a massive distraction and a huge expenditure of money and time to do it right. And frankly, at the early stages, the opportunity is limited. So my advice is to wait until you are solidly profitable and in the Harvest phase. To expand internationally prior to that stretches the company's resources at a time they will be stretched anyway, and it adds huge unnecessary risk without the promise of commensurate reward.

THE SCALE PHASE CHECKLIST

Scale, of course, is a relative term. One start-up may scale in a way that they grow to ten times their original size. Another start-up may scale so they're a hundred times bigger. Opportunities vary, so your scaling efforts need to be tailored to your particular situation. One of you may scale with great speed and in the most ambitious way possible, while another may expand slower and more modestly. There is no exact answer, and it depends on the founders, the market, and the opportunity.

Despite these differences, you all need to pay attention to the following issues as you scale:

- Have you figured out your business model; are you making sure you nail this model before you start to scale; does this model provide you with a way to generate significant revenue from the business?

- Are you scaling at the right time; are you making sure you're not moving too early (before you've nailed the business model) or too late?

- Are you willing to bring in new people with the specialized skills necessary to help the company succeed in its growing form? Are you also willing to make the right decisions about your current people (and yourself), insisting that they go from generalist to specialist and letting them go if they can't make the transition?

- Have you raised the necessary revenue to scale, either from increased revenues or from venture capital?

- Are you implementing processes to accommodate all the changes that are occurring as your company grows? Are these processes working? Are they helping coordinate efforts between expanded functions, and do they ensure efficient and effective communication and management?

- Have you spread the word through various marketing methods about your success in gaining customer traction?

- Are you resisting lowball offers? Do you understand the pitfalls of entertaining or accepting such offers?

- Even if you have plenty of money to expand your operations (through revenue or VC sources), are you holding off until you've carved out a significant share of market for your product and have achieved customer traction?

- Have you had tough conversations with cofounders or other key employees who are resisting new and more specialized roles in the growing company?

- Are you conscious of how the culture may be changing as you scale? Are you talking about what you want the culture to be as the company becomes bigger?

- Are you resisting the pressure to go global until you are fully scaled up and feeling super solid domestically?

HARVEST

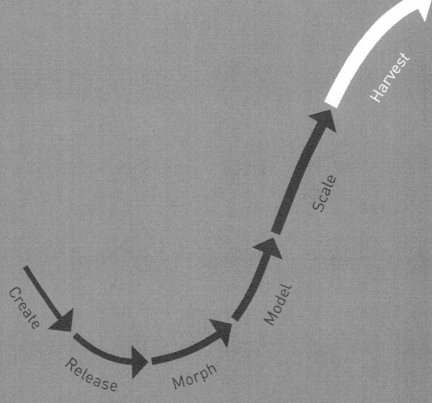

Create

Release

Morph

Model

Scale

Harvest

7

HARVEST:
THE JOY OF PUFFBALL DECISIONS

The Harvest phase is, in most respects, the easiest and the most enjoyable. It's primarily about capitalizing on the opportunity you have created by building a strong business. The decisions in this phase are certainly important but usually not life or death. David and I call them *puffball* decisions, where it's heads you win, tails you win more. You'll know you've moved from Scale to Harvest when your growth is starting to slow somewhat and you are generating substantial cash flow from operations. Personally, I love generating cash; it tends to relieve a huge amount of stress, it's a great place to be, and it offers independence. I am fond of saying, "If you are generating cash, you control your own destiny; if you are consuming cash, eventually someone else controls your destiny."

Once you are generating cash, you have a wonderful problem—you need to figure out what to do with it! A typical decision may involve whether to use your cash flow to invest in more revenue growth, to build up the company coffers, or to return money to the shareholders. Opportunities abound at this point in the life of a start-up, and they are opportunities you can do something about, because you now have the resources. The trick is to be disciplined.

However, the decisions you make here can be tough in ways that might not seem obvious initially. Yes, things are going well, but all sorts of issues around growth strategies will arise, and they have a huge impact on your company, not only now, but in the future.

Let's look at some of the key issues, starting with growth rate.

NOT TOO FAST, NOT TOO SLOW

No perfect rate of growth exists for all start-ups. Most companies have a natural rate of growth that matches the product with the opportunity and the company's ability to capture that opportunity. For a variety of reasons, some companies can grow much faster than others, and the rate of growth depends on the strength of the product and market, the strength of the business model, and the availability of viable marketing channels. What counts here is capital efficiency and disciplined capital allocation. Just because you have it doesn't mean you should spend it. In sales and marketing, for example, you may experience declining returns, meaning that the more you spend, the less effective the marketing dollars are. In the Harvest phase, the trick is to find the rate of growth that best fits the company. Rates of growth can vary based on a variety of factors, but you should have a sense of the rate that dovetails with your company's situation.

For instance, at FlexJobs, one of our many marketing strategies is to use search engine marketing (SEM) to acquire customers. But the universe of terms we can bid on is limited, both in quantity and effectiveness; the more we try to buy, the less effective this strategy becomes. The cost per acquisition is low initially but becomes increasingly expensive as we expand our reach. Because of declining returns, the cost of acquiring customers rises, and we reach a point where we can no longer acquire customers profitably. Some companies, however, rationalize the expense as a growth necessity and keep spending to bring in more customers. While this is occasionally acceptable in the Scale phase, it is a bad idea in the Harvest phase, especially when money should be spent on more effective growth initiatives or returned to shareholders.

Many entrepreneurs in the Harvest phase are overly infatuated with continued hypergrowth of 100 to 200 percent per year that is more appropriate in the Scale phase. As the company grows, its size will act as an anchor on the growth rate at some point. In many cases, it's better to grow at a more measured pace with internally generated funds. A measured pace also gives you financial flexibility to either handle unexpected setbacks, such as the loss of a major customer, or to take advantage of opportunities, such as acquiring new talent or even making an acquisition. Growing at a measured pace will also typically help you stay lean, focused, and disciplined. One of the primary dangers in the Harvest phase is that you start saying yes to too many things, especially to opportunities that are good but are not great. Steve Jobs once said, "People think focus means saying yes to the thing you've got to focus on. But that's not what it means at all. It means saying no to the hundred other good ideas that there are. You have to pick carefully. I'm actually as proud of the things we haven't done as the things I have done. Innovation is saying no to a thousand things."

Consider that the average company in the S&P 500 grows at about 5 percent per year. So if you are growing at 30 to 40 percent during the Harvest phase, you are knocking it out of the park. Grow at 30 percent annually over a sustained period of time and thanks to the magic of compounding (which I'll discuss later in the chapter), you will build a valuable enterprise and be a wealthy person. So grow at the right rate. Too fast and you are not spending efficiently, too slow and you are ceding opportunity to the competition.

TIME FOR PAYBACK

Start-up founders are responsible for compensating shareholders for their investment, whether it's funds angel investors put into the company or stock provided to employees as compensation for working there. When you accept investor money or offer stock as compensation to employees, an implicit obligation exists that at some point you'll provide liquidity so they can realize their investment return. Given that you've reached Harvest, the various liquidity options should start to open up. The most common options are the following:

- Launching an initial public offering (IPO)

- Selling the company

- Using share buybacks

- Paying dividends

An initial public offering (IPO) achieves two goals simultaneously: providing liquidity to shareholders and more cash for growth. It also requires adjustment to a new set of financial reporting responsibilities and obligations.

If you sell the company, you have a clean way to exit and provide liquidity. This is the optimal phase for being acquired, and it may be that this is right for you—you may be ready to get out and start something new. It's also possible that the acquisition deal calls for you to remain with the company. This is fine, though I've found that most start-up founders find it difficult to exist within a large corporate structure; within a year or two, they leave and create a new start-up.

If you have good cash flow, share buybacks help you keep ownership simple and corporate overhead low. Or you can pay dividends as a way to share the profits with shareholders while allowing them to also participate in the long-term value creation. Much of your decision depends on your and the shareholders' preferences as well as the company situation. There's no right way to create liquidity because everyone is different and responds to the outcomes of creating liquidity differently.

Launching An IPO

Many start-up founders view IPOs as a kind of Holy Grail, but in reality, they can create headaches for those founders who find the responsibilities that accompany being a public company irksome. For instance, entrepreneurs who hate paperwork and the minutiae of accounting (made vastly worse by the Sarbanes-Oxley laws, passed in the wake of the tech crash in 2000) noxious. In addition, being a public company isn't for everyone. Your performance is judged by every quarterly earnings report. Miss it once and your stock can lose 20 to 40 percent of its value, and you are probably going to get sued. The loss of paper profits can create morale problems, and headhunters can start poaching your people. If you miss earnings targets twice, stakeholders will clamor for a new CEO. After three misses, you are probably out of a job. Perhaps even worse, Wall Street's focus on short-term earnings can cause the management team to adopt this same focus. As a result, you will be tempted to make those quarterly reports look better—cutting expenses, including staff, and discounting your products—and end up hurting your long-term objectives. A great CEO like Jeff Bezos of Amazon is determined to avoid this trap, much to the chagrin of Wall Street analysts but to the great benefit of their long-term shareholders. But for every Jeff Bezos there are dozens of disillusioned CEOs who are victims of this insidious game.

Of course, an IPO may be your best option to raise funds for growth or to pay back your investors, so you have little choice but to move forward with this tactic. If you do an IPO, prepare to resist a short-term-only mentality and prepare for the tumult and intense scrutiny that can result when you become a public entity.

If the IPO scenario strikes you as horrifying or wrong for your business in other ways, you may want to pursue other options.

Selling the Company

If you decide to get acquired—a valid decision in the Harvest phase—keep in mind a few key points as you go through the process. First, keep the discussions limited to yourself and select members of the management team. Remember, selling the company can be incredibly distracting and disruptive. It's not the time to be transparent. While you may eventually open up the process, if the deal looks like it may go down, opening it up early is counterproductive.

Second, keep in mind the obvious, which is that the acquiring company is going to try to pay as little as possible. They can do this by lowballing or by grinding the price down in the due-diligence phase or by stretching out the payments over time. Stretching the payments over time is referred to as performance payments or *earn-outs*.

I'm not a fan of them, but sometimes they can't be avoided. If the acquiring company doesn't allow you the flexibility and resources required, then you are not going to be able to hit the performance goals. This needs to be included in the negotiations and contract.

Finally, be aware that the acquiring company will usually attempt to direct as much of the payment price toward management and away from the shareholders. This serves their purpose because they will need the management going forward but don't need the shareholders. It is your obligation to push back and strongly represent the shareholders' interests, establishing the buyout price for the shareholders first and only then discussing the management deal. The shareholders helped you reach this phase, you wouldn't exist without them, and you need to take care of them. In the long game, they will remember how they are treated, and you want that to be a pleasant memory. Your reputation will survive longer than the money. To grasp the business ethics involved, spend a Saturday afternoon reading Warren Buffett's letters to shareholders for his company Berkshire Hathaway. After reading five or ten of them, you'll know the right thing to do.

Share Buybacks

If you buy the shares back at the right price, it's a great way accommodating anyone who wants liquidity as well as those who wish to remain. For those shareholders who choose not to participate, their ownership of the company increases. I rarely tender my stock (recall my maxim, "you can't get rich selling"), since companies that can buy shares back are usually doing pretty well. In fact, I have often purchased more stock along with the company. When it comes to good companies, I agree with Warren Buffet when he quoted Mae West: "Too much of a good thing can be wonderful!"

Dividends

While dividends are not exactly a liquidity option, they can be a great way to provide a return to investors, as long as the company has all the resources it needs to continue growing. The best way to distribute excess cash is if the corporate structure is a Sub-S or LLC, which allows the excess cash to be distributed to investors without being taxed at the corporate level. Note that these structures also require you to pay your individual portion of the tax due on the overall profits whether they are distributed or not, so make sure to discuss this in depth with your accountant.

WHAT TO DO WITH YOUR EXCESS CASH

Let's assume for the moment that you're not going to sell the company; you want to continue to run and grow it. Unlike the previous Scale phase—where your expenses equaled or surpassed your revenue—you now have the luxury of revenues exceeding your expenses. This excess cash provides you with the opportunity to pursue a number of positive growth strategies. Let's look at each and what they entail.

Create New Products

Ultimately, new products are usually the core growth driver. You now have infrastructure in place that will streamline the development, marketing, and distribution of new product initiatives. The trick is to figure out your infrastructure's unique advantages and leverage them. Once Microsoft dominated the market for operating systems, they began introducing applications such as Excel, Word, and PowerPoint. Those products got fantastic leverage from the fact that Microsoft (1) had a very talented engineering staff, (2) sold through the same distribution channels, (3) possessed a well-developed marketing channel, and (4) were privy to upcoming improvements in the operating system and so were best positioned to make use of them. I'll talk more about how to optimize new product development in a larger company later in the book. For a late stage start-up, you need to do it with small, isolated, and dedicated teams, and they will need to start at the beginning of the J Curve.

Invest in the Brand

When executed well, the brand helps attract customers, but more than that, it insulates it or at least provides a certain measure of protection against economic swings, competitors' new products, and so on. In consumer-facing products, building the brand is essential (in the vodka category, for instance, brand is probably 85 percent of what makes the business tick), but a strong brand can also be useful in the business-to-business sector. Investing in the brand can mean everything from spending money on traditional media advertising to social media efforts to public relations campaigns.

Expand Globally

As I said earlier, I believe that generally it's a mistake to go global during the previous Scale phase, primarily because too many other key activities require your time, money, and attention. This strain can put you in a precarious position if the domestic business stumbles in any way. The Harvest phase, however, is the perfect time to expand internationally. You have the cash and the bandwidth, and you're looking for the next mountain to conquer. Since international sales can be over half of your eventual sales, it's a real opportunity, and you want to take global opportunities seriously.

Acquisitions

This one comes with a warning sticker: *Be wary of big or equal acquisitions*. Being in a position to buy another company is exciting, and it may sound even more exciting to make a splash with a high-profile acquisition. But temper your excitement with clear-eyed reality: Most large acquisitions fail to deliver on their promise. Despite good intentions, it's tough to mesh two different product lines and cultures together. Of course, pre-acquisition, managements and their advisers see only tremendous synergies between the two companies. I highly distrust the word *synergy*, because the vaunted synergies rarely materialize, and if they do, they are almost always way smaller than expected. Further, the enthusiasm for these synergies can divert attention from what can go wrong. If you recall, one of the most well-known recent acquisitions—Hewlett Packard's purchase of Compaq—was announced with lots of positive adjectives: bold, game-changer, and visionary. While the investment bankers made good money on the deal, nearly everyone else involved lost money; and Hewlett Packard CEO, Carly Fiorina, lost her job.

Be even more wary of acquisitions for strategic reasons or a merger of equals. In the former instance, if you have to spend a lot of money to obtain a better strategy, then you probably aren't in great shape and no acquisition will help you. In the latter situation, if someone even utters the phrase *merger of equals*, run for the hills; the combined companies will create clashes and stalemates for cultural and other reasons that can't be resolved because power is evenly split.

On the positive side, doing acquisitions for your company can be a viable strategy in the Harvest phase if you follow this guideline: The smaller the acquisition is relative to the size of the acquirer, the better. As a corollary to this guideline: The targeted company needs to be big enough and offer sufficient upside to justify the investment of money and time. So there's a sweet spot between too small and too big that you need to shoot for if you plan on spending your Harvest money in this way. Acquisitions where technology, products, or people are acquired tend to do well. Companies such as Cisco are brilliant at making small acquisitions that have fueled their growth. Others, such as Apple with its purchase of Next Computer (1997), helped them acquire technology for their future operating system as well as talent—it brought Steve Jobs back into the fold. Apple subsequently acquired core technology and people for the iPod (SoundJam MP, 2000), for voice control software (Siri, 2010), head-phones and accessories (Beats, 2014), and many other key product breakthroughs. In all, Apple has done over seventy acquisitions, but rarely paid more than 1 percent of their market cap at the time (Next being an exception). Cisco has done over two hundred acquisitions, but again, rarely paid more than 2 percent of the Cisco market cap for any single one.

THE FOREVER START-UP

I borrowed the modifier from Warren Buffett, who describes this preferred holding period as "forever." While I recognize that many investors thirst for liquidity—they want to sell what they bought in order to realize their investment return and use the money for other ventures or purposes—I have found great value and satisfaction in staying with the start-up as it grows and matures.

In Harvest, you may find yourself trying to figure out if you should sell or stay. Let me give you two admittedly biased reasons for considering the latter seriously.

First, consider that you have suffered through the long, cold winter of the early J Curve. To use another metaphor, you've paid your dues. Having been through tough times and knowing how difficult it is to achieve start-up success, why not relish the Harvest phase and beyond? You may find great satisfaction in running and growing a successful company, especially given the struggle you went through to get to that point. Therefore, don't dismiss the possibility of staying with the company for an extended period of time. As tempting as Harvest liquidity is, you may find that embarking on a growth strategy and generating more revenue is what matters to you, and becoming a serial entrepreneur and bouncing from one venture to the next is less satisfying. If you think you are anxious to begin another start-up, remind yourself that the bottom of that J Curve is very tough and that more than half of start-ups fail. Every start-up founder has different needs and goals, so this is a time to consider what yours are.

Second, holding on to your start-up company for a long time also confers the benefit of compounding. Albert Einstein declared, "Compound interest is the eighth wonder of the world. He who understands it, earns it. He who doesn't . . . pays it." For whatever reason, I've observed that most start-up founders and investors in general don't recognize the importance of compounding. Maybe it's that they're innately present oriented, or perhaps it's their short attention span or propensity for action (an expensive habit in investing), but many times their reflex is to get in and then get out.

I suspect it's just plain hard for our human minds to grasp the power of compounding (unless you're Einstein). Consider the story of the rice and the chessboard. Legend has it that the inventor of chess showed the game to the emperor of India. The emperor was incredibly impressed and told the inventor to name his reward. The inventor responded, "I only wish for this: Give me one grain of rice for the first square of the chessboard, two grains for the next square, four grains for the next . . ." The inventor requested a doubling of the amount of rice for each successive square—a chessboard has six-ty-four squares. Seems cheap, right? The emperor though so too and quickly agreed to the inventor's request, thinking to himself that the inventor was foolish to accept such a meager reward. After a week of study, though, the emperor's treasurer told him that in reality, the amount of rice would constitute an astronomical sum that would take the country many years to produce—eighteen trillion grains of rice, to be precise. Thus, the value of compounding becomes clear. Though, as a side note, the emperor was furious with the inventor for "deceiving" him, and he chopped off his head—perhaps there's a lesson there for inventors and start-ups about being careful what you ask for.

The two primary variables that affect the compound interest equa-tion are length of time and rate of return. In a start-up, your rate of return is the result of your daily efforts, and let's assume you're doing everything you can to grow the business. The second variable is time, and time is the pixie dust that creates compound interest magic.

Compounding over the short term doesn't work in the short term, as the results are limited, but compounding over a long period of time is indeed the "eighth wonder of the world," as Einstein referred to it. In my view, long-term tax-deferred compounding is where real wealth is created.

Here's a statistic that will stop and make you think before you cash in your successful start-up: The average amount of time the top thirty billionaires on the Forbes 400 list have held their primary holding is over thirty years. I'm a big fan of Warren Buffett, and I've spent a lot of time studying what makes him and his partner, Charlie Munger, so uniquely good at investing. One of the most overlooked and underrated aspects of their investing style is their long-term holding strategy; the average holding period of Berkshire's top six holdings from 1977 to 2009 was twenty years (http://www.fool. com/investing/general/2014/08/17/warren-buffetts-staggering-success-rests-on-this-1.aspx). Of course, holding for the long term presupposes that you have a great business. If you have a lousy business, time will not be your friend, and you have two choices: Either make it a better one or sell it ASAP.

DO YOU HAVE A GREAT BUSINESS?

If you decide in the Harvest phase that you want to create and run a sustainable enterprise, then analyze whether you have a great business—great companies are the ones that possess the capacity to be sustainable and the ones that you never want to let go of. Here are the four traits you can use to identify whether you have a great long-term business.

A Protective Moat

In other words, a company has created a surrounding shield that provides them with a degree of safety from competitive threats and also gives them pricing power. Railroads are a great example of companies that have these moats. They serve a valuable purpose— transporting a significant percentage of food and other products to markets throughout the US. They also have an infrastructure with which few companies can compete—a network of tracks, the associated land rights, plus the trains and other capital equipment that cost billions of dollars. I wouldn't want to start a new railroad company to compete with the existing ones. While you may not be able to build as deep and wide a moat as this one, you can ask yourself the previous question to ascertain if you have a moat: Would you want to start a new company to compete with your existing start-up? Here are some companies I would not want to compete with: eBay, Facebook, Twitter, Amazon, or Coke. As Buffett once said: "If you gave me a billion dollars to compete with Coke, I would have to give it back." Buffett realizes that a billion dollars is not going to get you over the moat of the Coke brand value and distribution.

Smart and Competent Management

Smart and competent management that is passionate about the company's mission, act like owners, and treat their shareholders like partners. Take a cue from the tech world, where many founders still lead the largest companies. Jeff Bezos of Amazon, Larry Ellison at Oracle, Sergey Brin and Larry Page of Google, and Mark Zuckerberg of Facebook are some examples. These are long-term thinkers and strategists, and like Bezos, are well known for resisting Wall Street's demands for short-term results in favor of long-term strategy. These founders care more about their company mission than the money they are making.

Ability to Withstand Sudden Technological Change

No doubt you've heard of companies that were destroyed or debilitated by rapidly emerging new technologies. Blackberry is a great example of a once-dominant product that got trounced by new technology, the smart phone. If you're vulnerable to this sudden shift, you're going to struggle because technological breakthroughs will happen with increasing frequency. Some companies are impervious to these changes because technology is not a major factor in their business: Coca Cola probably isn't going to lose market share as a new generation of mobile phones emerge. If technology does affect your business, then you need to possess the in-house capacity and, perhaps, most importantly, the culture to anticipate and capitalize on changing technologies.

A High Return on Equity

Return on equity measures how much profit a company can make relative to the money that has been invested. The airline business, for instance, has a poor return on equity. An airline is required to keep purchasing expensive airplanes and maintaining them in order to have any business at all, and there is so much competition that it's hard to get a return on those investments. A study done by the National Bureau of Economic Research found that the airline industry lost money in twenty-three out of thirty-one years since deregulation (http://www.nber.org/papers/w16744.pdf). It's been postulated that if you add up the cumulative profits of the airline industry since the Wright Brothers, the result is less than zero. Return on equity is tied directly back to the strength of the business model. Airlines have almost no moat, high capital requirements, high labor costs, little price leverage, extreme complexity, high frictional scaling, and a lot of competition; you want the reverse. A great business model will get you great returns on investments made in that business.

ANALYZING SPINOFF POSSIBILITIES

During the Harvest phase, you may also find yourself with the opportunity to spin off a business. As the company moves through each of the phases, you may naturally develop new products. The majority of these products will complement each other; synergies exist between product lines, and you can share people and other resources easily. One of the products, however, may be so sufficiently different from the others that it requires a greater degree of independence in order to reach its potential. You realize that everyone would benefit a lot more if it were spun off from the company rather than allowed to exist within it.

David, my business partner, and I learned the value of spinoffs when Sam Shank approached us about spinning off HotelTonight from DealBase. At first I resisted his suggestion, making the argument that because both companies were in the travel business, they belonged under the same roof. Sam argued that it was going to require substantial financing to get HotelTonight going, and the existing DealBase business confused the story in a number of ways. Running DealBase was going to be a distraction at a time that HotelTonight was going to require 100 percent focus. According to Sam, financing and managing them both under the same corporate umbrella would be tricky. When Sam received a term sheet from Battery Ventures for funding the spinout, it was proof that Sam was probably right. All I can say is thank God I didn't let my stubbornness get the best of me. Sam was entirely correct: Once HotelTonight was spun off, it took off! Moreover, DealBase continues to thrive under the incredibly capable leadership of Clem Bason and his talented team. The positive experience opened our eyes to the potential benefits of spinoffs.

Here's a good analogy from the world of gambling to use when thinking about whether you have a product that qualifies for a spinoff. David and I refer to this analogy as *splitting aces*. In the blackjack card game, when you are dealt two aces to start, the proper response is to split them because they are much stronger as separate hands than together; the odds increase that one or both of your hands will be a winner. If your first two cards are a pair of fives, however, you don't want to split them because they constitute a good hand together, but apart they are weak.

The questions to ask yourself in Harvest, therefore, are whether you have two products or businesses that are aces as opposed to fives. And would they operate more effectively apart than together?

Launching a spinoff is easier than you may think. It requires you to mirror the cap table (the cap table reflects the equity ownership of the company), add in an option pool for management, and provide for initial funding. You also need to make sure you have a great CEO for both companies; it's not worth doing before you do. We have found that you can find amazing candidates to become CEO if the search is thorough. Being a CEO is considered the pinnacle of a career, so you can generate a lot of interest from experienced and incredibly talented individuals by offering the top spot. It's a great deal for prospective CEOs, since they're going to be handed a business that is already up and running, saving them the uncertainty and perils of the long, cold winter of the J Curve.

David and I have had great success with our spinoffs—most are still operational and thriving. As much as I would like to attribute this to our acumen, I've found that spinoffs often do well if the circumstances are right (great product, good CEO, good financials, etc.). The success rate is far higher than starting an enterprise from scratch, and that is primarily due to the fact that the spinoff has, in most cases, already made it through the long, cold winter that is the trough of the J curve.

When you look at a spinoff as a start-up, it has huge advantages over a raw start-up, usually because it has a sort of running start. The product is probably already built and released (Create and Release phases), the core management team may already be in place, you may already have customer traction and product/market fit (Morph), and the business model may be in place (Model). As such, you just may have skipped the first four phases of the J curve—the most challenging and risky phases of the process. In some instances, you may have to refine some of the phases, but the process is still much faster than if you're starting from scratch.

It's worth noting that, historically, spinoffs of public companies also tend to work out well. For example, Barry Diller at IAC/InterActive has made an art form out of it and has delivered superior shareholder value in doing so. Public company spinouts do so well in large part because they receive the dedication, focus, passion, and funding as an independent entity that they did not receive when they were part of the parent company. In short, they get love!

THE HARVEST PHASE CHECKLIST

Perhaps the biggest item on the checklist is whether you stay or go—retain ownership of the business and grow it, or sell it and move on to another venture. But within this major Harvest decision are a number of smaller but crucial options and tasks that will determine your start-up's fate, not only now but in the future. Therefore, use the following questions to address these issues:

- Are you growing your company at a rate that is well suited to your resources, goals, and competitive framework?

- How are you returning money to those who invested in your company—IPO, selling the company, share buybacks, or dividends? Have you thought long and hard about the ramifications of each option and which one is best for you?

- If you have excess cash flow, are you spending it wisely and strategically? Are you investing in the brand, growing globally, making an acquisition, or creating new products? Have you weighed the pros and cons of each spending option and picked the one that fits with your start-up's situation?

- Have you seriously considered holding on to the company you started and staying with it for the long term (as opposed to selling reflexively upon reaching this phase)? Have you assessed whether you would gain greater satisfaction from creating a successful, sustainable organization or starting a new company from scratch? Have you projected the effect that tax-deferred compounding might have on the value of your company over a lengthy period of time?

- How do the long-term prospects of your company rate on four key factors: a protective moat, skilled, passionate management, ability to withstand technological change, and a high return on equity?

- Do you possess a second (or third or fourth) product that is a good candidate for a spinoff?

8

RAISING DOLLARS FOR START-UPS: A PHASE-BY-PHASE GUIDE

No matter what phase of the J Curve you happen to be in, money is usually an issue and is often on your mind. Not having enough money is a real and palpable fear of most start-ups. The good news is that most founders need less than they think, and ironically, more advantages exist to having too little than having too much. Every start-up I can remember has complained about possessing limited resources, but what founders don't realize is that scarcity forces you to focus, make disciplined choices, and move quickly. And these are prerequisite behaviors if you are going to make it through the long, cold winter of the J Curve.

I've seen few companies die because of a lack of resources. While many do run out of money eventually, the cause of their demise usually has little to do with adequate funding. I struggle to think of a single start-up that died when more money would have made a difference. The truth is that most companies die because they fail to make a great product that the market cares about. When a company that we have a significant investment in runs out of money, David and I usually dig in our pockets for one final infusion of funds, even though we may have serious doubts. The last investment is usually to confirm what was already obvious—the company isn't going to make it, and money ain't the issue.

As an aside, I'll point out that in my experience, the two greatest fears that founders tend to have is 1) that they are going to run out of money—you could call this fear of asphyxiation, and 2) that they will get clobbered by a competitor—you could call this fear of being murdered. But the vast majority of companies die from neither; their demise is the result of self-inflicted wounds. Sam Altman observed that "99% of startups die from suicide, not murder" (Sam Altman's Playbook Blog). I would add, neither do they die from asphyxiation—as long as they are smart about how they handle their finances.

Finance issues vary by phases and by specific situations, but they often seem omnipresent, and how you deal with these issues can have a meaningful impact on your start-up, both in the short term and long term. Though I've touched on some of these matters in the earlier phase chapters, we need to look at them in greater depth to understand their implications for your business as well as the best ways to deal with them when they arise.

To get you in the right frame of mind for this discussion, think about the start-up journey as analogous to a desert crossing. In this analogy, water is the equivalent of money—it is what will sustain you during the journey. You possess only enough water to reach the next oasis. To manage your water usage effectively, you must build in a margin of error, knowing that delays and mistakes will occur along the way. To assume a perfect crossing—that everything goes according to plan—is dangerous. If you are only halfway to the next oasis and you start running low on water, you're probably going to panic and react without thinking. You might overuse the water or parcel it out in such small increments that it fails to sustain you. The goal is to manage your water astutely and conservatively, recognizing that once you make it through the initial four phases of the J Curve, you'll reach a land where water is plentiful, and eventually, you'll own the wells that produce the water, and you can draw from them liberally.

RAMEN PROFITABILITY: THE VALUE OF HAVING JUST ENOUGH MONEY

While most start-up founders fear running short of cash, few worry about having an overabundance of funds. In fact, both are legitimate fears. To address these fears, recognize that start-ups (almost) always work with limited resources. That just goes with the territory. Having minimally sufficient funds engenders good behaviors: You are forced to focus on mission-critical matters, work hard, and make quick decisions. It keeps you lean and fast, two essential qualities during the early phases. These are the behaviors that will help you make it through the aforementioned desert—or, to recall our earlier metaphor, to survive the long, cold winter (the trough) of the J Curve.

Paradoxically, few companies perish because of a lack of cash, but many perish because they have too much. What matters is how they use their available resources. If you move through the phases of the J Curve effectively—if you accomplish each phase's tasks in the right order and the right way—you'll minimize the lean phases two through four, which will greatly reduce the financial burden of the journey.

In many ways, a bigger problem is having too much money, especially too much money too soon. Too much money leads to bad habits, the chief ones being sloppiness and lack of discipline. In chapter 5, I described the tech blog GigaOM and how they raised $20 million and scaled prematurely, attempting to become a combination tech blog and conference and research business before any of the individual business lines had a working business model. Scaling before nailing the model, they went bust.

We helped one of our start-ups, Knowingly, purchase GigaOM's assets from the creditors, so we have some insight into the financial issues that led to their failure. We discovered that GigaOM's sprawling offices in San Francisco and Manhattan cost $60,000 monthly, that the San Francisco office included a $2,000 coffee maker, and that they had a high-paid editorial staff of twenty-two people and ten product-development employees. While the conference business might have been making some money, the blog and research businesses were not. They had fallen into the dangerous trap of believing that each part of the business was required to keep the other parts going. But since none of the parts of the business was making money, this thinking only increased the losses. GigaOM could have been profitable if they had been far more rigorous in controlling expenses, but they started spending and expanding before they had a solid business model that would support this growth. Note that the actual product—the writers, the conferences, and the research—were excellent. But because the company had too much money, it was never forced to make the numbers work. And trust me, in the end, more money was definitely not going to help.

When I think about that $2,000 coffee maker (which is painful to even contemplate a start-up having), I contrast it with the concept of *ramen profitability*. Ramen profitability is defined as the start-up team's ability to make sufficient revenue to sustain itself on a ramen noodle diet. As Y Combinator cofounder Paul Graham points out in his post on this subject (http://www.paulgraham.com/ramen-profitable.html), becoming ramen profitable has a number of distinct advantages: (1) you have proven that you have a product that people will pay money for; (2) you don't need to raise money, which means you can spend more time focused on the product; and (3) you and your team get a huge morale boost because you don't have the Damoclean sword of losing money hanging over your head, and suddenly you are legit—a real business making real money. All three of these make it much easier to raise money when you decide to because you have addressed many of the primary fears of an investor, and you are on the right side of the timeless paradox of fund-raising that "It's easier to raise money when you don't need it."

Working from a place of scarcity rather than plenty encourages resourcefulness; it forces you to look for leverage. When I started LoveToKnow, the dot-com crash was at its worst. Like many tech investors at the time, I had torched the better part of whatever fortune I had built up to that point. So the capital available to start a new enterprise was limited. I required engineers to develop the product I envisioned, but I couldn't pay Silicon Valley prices for tech experts. So I was forced to search elsewhere, and my initial hires were in India, where talent was available at a fraction of the US price. When I was finally able to afford to hire in the US, I initially did so on a part-time basis. I didn't want the monthly expense of having a physical office, and I theorized that not having one would allow us to access talent from virtually anywhere in the country or the world. We focused on creating a viable, virtual company and discovered many practices that made working virtually productive and rewarding. It was such an effective approach that over a decade later, we still don't have an office. And we discovered so much talent willing to work from home that we helped Sara Sutton Fell start FlexJobs to connect that workforce with great opportunities. Without our lean circumstances, these positive events probably would not have happened and we may not have made it.

By working with a severely limited budget, I had to scramble to find the help I needed. It forced us to adopt good habits and even to discover some novel business practices that would prove to be valuable long term. Most importantly, keeping costs low bought me time—time that we needed to figure out both the product and the business model. That is a good thing because my brilliant, original idea was a flop. We weren't successful until the third morph. I'm not suggesting that every start-up founder should live like a monk for years in order to save every penny possible. Instead, adapt the ramen model to your own particular situation and needs.

My company, for instance, became Howard-ramen profitable, which had to include a family sized budget, food that was a cut or two above ramen noodles, and my love for good wine. I did, however, keep costs down whenever I could, and I was able to reinvest the cash flow in growing the business, thus bootstrapping its growth. As a result, we never had to raise outside capital. More to the point, the company adopted a relatively frugal mindset, improving our chances of survival when we hit the inevitable rough spots. It created a discipline that shaped our structure and practices, and we have maintained that discipline to this day.

Admittedly, some exceptions to the ramen principle exist, but generally, I would heed the words of the Roman philosopher Seneca: "The less money, the less trouble..." While you need a certain amount of money to get started and see you through the phases, you probably need far less than you think. If you have a good initial idea and the ability to sell it, you should be able to raise at least some money (and if you can't, it may be a red flag that there's something wrong with the idea or how you're presenting it). But let's say you believe the prospective investors who turn you down are wrong, and you are absolutely convinced you're on to something big. Then, you have the option of creating the start-up on a shoestring and trusting that either your product will generate the revenue you need or that you'll reach a point where a degree of success convinces investors to reconsider.

HOW TO RAISE MONEY THE HARD WAY

Raising money is a difficult undertaking, and it takes a huge amount of time and effort. If selling doesn't come naturally, then it's going to be twice as hard. People aren't just going to hand over big bucks because you've asked them for it, especially if you're not a skilled salesperson. Perhaps the biggest mistake start-up founders make is thinking that it's going to be easy to bring in funding and that investors would have to be brain-dead to pass on such a terrific opportunity.

Some start-up founders don't put much time or effort into their presentation. They don't visit enough potential investors or different types of investors. They don't keep at it long enough. And when the money doesn't pour into their coffers immediately, they become discouraged and stop trying.

If, on the other hand, you accept that the task before you is a challenging one, you'll approach this task with energy and commitment. Here are some basic guidelines that will facilitate your fund-raising efforts:

- Plan how you'll raise money and run the business concurrently. Raising money can and should be all consuming. It requires significant amounts of time and energy, leaving you with precious little of either to manage daily business tasks. Ideally, you have a cofounder, and one of you focuses on raising money and the other on running the business. If not, you will probably need to delegate business functions to someone else while you raise money. If you can't delegate, then you should probably accept that business progress is going to slow down or stop while you are shaking the bushes for money.

- Generate interest among multiple parties simultaneously. You don't want interest trickling in, which is what will happen if you move sequentially and methodically from one investing source to the next, allowing too much time to elapse between visits. Ideally, you'll choreograph the process so you generate interest from a variety of sources at roughly the same time. In this way, you produce a groundswell of interest and force investors to compete with one another. Investors hate being the first one to commit, but they also hate missing out on a hot deal, and bringing together multiple parties with interest at the same time will allow the latter reality to overcome the former.

- Approach raising money as a numbers game. You may believe you only need to meet with five investors and you'll obtain the money you need. Instead, thirty is a more realistic number. If you target thirty investors, you'll probably end up meeting with fifteen of them face-to-face, and then the odds are decent that one of them, or maybe even a few of them, will invest in your start-up. If no one chooses to invest even though you've knocked on a lot of doors, consider that this may be a sign that your start-up is missing something.

People become investors in start-ups because they have money. They usually have money because they earned it the hard way (I've rarely seen inherited money invested in start-ups). If people have earned enough money the hard way to be in a position to invest, then their business judgment is usually pretty good. In fact, one of the great benefits that you derive from fund-raising meetings is free consulting—as part of your discussion, investors will usually tell you what they like and what they don't like. The commentary is not always on point because investors may not be as familiar with your particular market and opportunity as you are, but it's a good test. Again, if none of these business-savvy people will invest, then it's worth taking a hard look at your idea. If you still love it and you're convinced it's viable despite all the naysayers, you will need to bootstrap it.

BOOTSTRAPPING

If you can't raise money, or don't want to, you can attempt a bootstrap. In a bootstrapping situation, you provide the initial capital, and once it gets going, your start-up is responsible for funding itself. This method holds a special place in my heart because I've been forced to do it so often. I'm not the world's greatest salesperson, and I really dislike fund-raising. Investors also usually hate my initial ideas. When investors think my ideas are bad, I usually think they are wrong and delight in proving it to them. I also have a great appreciation of the substantial positives that come from the simplicity of either owning something outright or with a small group of trusted partners. In addition, I like that bootstrapping forces extreme financial discipline—spending your own money makes you highly conscious of every dollar that comes in or goes out.

One word of warning, I don't in any way condone putting yourself in a situation of extreme financial risk. You've worked hard for your savings; be prudent about dipping into it. Consider that it is likely you will lose money. Of course, you hope (and I hope) you will not, but keep in mind that statistically there is a good likelihood your investment could end up a zero. Never, ever put your own health or your family's welfare at risk. As the famous TV detective character Tony Baretta once famously quipped: "Don't roll the dice, if you can't pay the price!"

But if bootstrapping is your only alternative and you've decided you can afford the investment, embrace it with pride. It's entirely possible to succeed with this approach—much more possible than a lot of people might imagine—and here are some tips that will increase your chances of success:

- Identify how much cash you can scrounge from various sources. This includes credit cards, home mortgage, and savings. This is the total amount that's available to you for investing in your start-up.

- Divide this total by two; this is the amount you have available to bootstrap.

- The other half of the total can be used as a buffer in case the business starts going south; it may also be used if the initial investment is gone and you remain convinced that your idea will work. Before using this second tranche, make sure you can afford to lose it without impacting your health, marriage, or family. To repeat what should be obvious, nothing (not even a good start-up) is worth sacrificing your health, marriage, or family.

- Consider working at a day job while getting the start-up going. While this limits the amount of time you can spend on the start-up, it provides you with a source of income that can be beneficial psychologically as well as from a cash flow standpoint. The good news is that you'll have more time than founders who have investors—you won't have to spend time fund-raising or providing financial updates.

- Spend the least amount possible to get to revenue as fast as possible. This is the magic formula to bootstrapping success. Move through the phases with maximum efficiency until you reach real revenue.

Ingenuity helps bootstrappers a lot. When I started my first company, Inmark Development, with my original cofounder, Cliff Ribaudo, we worked out of a room in his parents' house until we had the product nearly completed, then we got a small office. After two years, we raised $250,000 from investors, including one of our customers in Luxembourg (a side note—money often arrives from strange places). We promptly torched all of it on questionable hires and even more questionable product features, forcing us back to bootstrapping mode. In that mode, we requested that our larger customers pay upfront for features they wanted. Our monthly expenses were $35,000, and we would create whatever features our customers desired if they'd advance us the money so we could cover our operating expenses.

It was a ragged path to profitability, but it was one that a lot of bootstrappers travel. One bonus of this method is that you'll end up owning a lot more of your company this way than if you have multiple funding rounds.

PHASE-BY-PHASE FINANCIAL FOCUS

Within each of the phase chapters, I touched on key financial topics, but you could easily write an entire book on each of these topics alone, so I know unanswered questions exist. Because money is a constant and wide-ranging concern for start-up founders, this is an opportunity to delve a bit deeper into the issues you'll confront as you move through the phases.

Create

As you now know, I believe it's much easier to raise money in this initial phase than it is later, when the numbers trickle in and may not inspire the same confidence as your vision and strategic statement. The J Curve predicts an initial downswing as you move forward, so recognize that six to twelve months down the road, it's likely to be much more difficult to induce anyone to invest. It often isn't until Model or Scale that fund-raising becomes easier than it is in Create, so get the money you can while you can, keep expenses low, and focus on reaching the Scale phase.

When raising money in the Create phase, understand the incentives and inclinations of your prospective investors. They are going to be inclined to take a wait-and-see attitude before committing dollars to you; they are always hoping for more data to convince them you're on to something. They believe time works in their favor because the price doesn't change, but they get more data as time goes on. They tend to carry a fear that they will look foolish if they jump in and nobody else does. I call this *fear of looking stupid* (FOLS). They will tend to equivocate and delay.

The way to jar these investors out of their wait-and-see mindset is by moving them from FOLS to FOMO. FOMO stands for *fear of missing out,* and it's a primary motivator for investors. You create FOMO by securing the interest of multiple parties at the same time. FOMO is the reason that the fastest money to come into a start-up is always the last 20 percent, and it's also the easiest; it can come in via a single phone call from a fence-sitter. The first 20 percent, by contrast, is tough, primarily because of FOLS. It tends to trickle in over a period of months. One way to combat the FOLS versus FOMO is to offer a discount to investors who commit first. I've seen some deals where the company gives a discount of 10 to 20 percent to the first group of investors to commit, and I think it's smart. Even though, as an investor, I bristle at it if I'm in the nondiscounted group, I do understand it and think it can be an effective motivator.

Release

It can take time for a product to generate revenue, so once again, watching expenses is key. Most people assume that after they release the product, it will become easier to raise money, and they'll soon start generating money from sales. Both assumptions are often incorrect, at least for a lengthy period of time. You're also incorrect if you believe your company should receive a higher valuation because you're one step ahead of where you were when you first started fund-raising—you have a real product out there in real customers' hands. While it's true that having a product is indeed an accomplishment and it does prove the team's ability to create what was only discussed before, it often doesn't justify much of an increase in valuation. That may sound disappointing, but the reality is that it's tough to justify a significant step up in valuation until you demonstrate significant customer traction. In fact, when you're still in the Release phase, I'd ignore fund-raising altogether to save the time and avoid the distraction. That it will take multiple iterations and morphs to get liftoff for your product means you will want as much runway as possible. So keeping expenses low becomes the overarching priority for this phase. Skip the launch party. Refuse to hire more developers. Be your own sales force; even if you're not the best salesperson, your product needs to be so obviously good that it overcomes any lack of sales ability. Don't succumb to the belief that a few more marketing dollars will get the sales wheel spinning. Focus on getting the product right, and realize that it's a marathon, not a sprint.

Morph

Again, this is not a great time to be raising money for a variety of reasons. If you do need additional funds, my suggestion is to go back to your existing investors—you don't have to spend a lot of time making your pitch to people who know you. But I would not spend a lot of time looking for new investors in this phase—wait until you get significant customer traction at least, or even better, until you nail the business model before reaching beyond current investors.

In this Morph phase, time is money—it takes a lot of time to get to product/market fit, almost always much longer than expected. So you want to do everything you can to save time. Here are six suggestions:

1. Don't be stubborn.

2. Be intellectually honest, brutally honest, with yourself and your team. If you are in denial about the current product

iteration, then you're spending too much time and money on it, and you're torching the funds you will need to move on to the iteration that customers will love. Force yourself to view each morph objectively, and if it's not working, move on.

3. Keep things lean. Agility counts, and a smaller developmental team can adjust and iterate faster than a large one. And, of course, a smaller team is less expensive.

4. Become an A-plus tester. Being astute about testing your products will help you grasp market reaction fast and accurately. Listen closely and without bias to the data—let it tell you what to do next, and respond quickly.

5. Avoid the more money trap. You convince yourself that if you can raise x dollars, you'll have what you need to create the breakthrough you crave. In reality, you'll probably spend inordinate amounts of time trying to raise x dollars rather than concentrating on getting the product right. If you absolutely must have more money, shoot for the minimum so you can raise it quickly and get back to the morphing task at hand.

6. Iterate fast. Keep the iterations moving. If your product is web based, think about getting a new version out in days, not weeks. Your money is waiting for you once you find the winning product, and the only way to find it is to keep iterating and morphing until your product resonates with customers.

Model

The Model phase focuses on getting the financial model of the business right. While it usually does not take as long as the previous phases to perfect, it can, and, as such, you still need to be conservative with your cash. The good news is that once you nail this, the funding will become quite a bit easier. And if you have indeed nailed the model, then you should have some cash coming in from sales. If you are going to require more funding, then you can begin those discussions during this phase. Since you have the product and customer traction, your story is starting to come together for the next funding. Securing a round of funding takes a long time, so it's OK to ramp up discussions a little before every duck is in line. Going forward, your story should be improving as revenue should start flowing in. You can start with the preliminary work, such as researching what funding sources may be interested. Then reach out to them, work to schedule meetings, and have preliminary discussions to gauge their interest.

Scale

Scaling is expensive, so if you are taking outside capital, now is the time to bring in the real money. As I noted in the Scale chapter, you have a number of options here: venture capital firms, banks, and strategic partners.

Again, classic venture capitalists are focused primarily on scaling opportunities, and they are generally good at it. Once upon a time, VCs used to take more product, team, business model, and market risks. While they will still claim to do that, the reality is that the vast bulk of their investments are made to Scale businesses that have made it through the first three to four phases of the J Curve. They correctly realize that most of the risk exists in that tough part of the

J Curve, so they avoid it, or they make relatively small placeholder-type bets in those early phases. The good news is that if you have made it through the long, cold winter of the nadir of the J Curve and are now solidly moving into the Scale phase, you are talking their language. You are exactly what they want, so by all means, you should go and pitch them. The pitch that classic venture firms love is, *We have an amazing product, a huge market, and a massive customer adoption. Plus, we just turned on the revenue model, and it's working. We're looking for some money to make this a much bigger enterprise. If you really have that in a convincing way, the VCs will practically lock the conference room doors and do a deal with you on the spot.*

VCs are thirsty for those types of situations, and again, even if they say no, you will often get some solid advice from them. If you do decide to go for formal venture capital, remember that they are going to be your partner for a long time, so make sure it's a partner you really want on board and is a good fit for you and your company.

Of course, you may not need or want venture money, and it may not be a good fit for your long-term vision. Often, there is no imperative to grow at a sky-high rate during Scale. You may be in the enviable position of being able to fund some if not all of your growth through your cash flow; this method also tends to instill financial and operational discipline and avoids dilution for the existing shareholders. If, on the other hand, you aren't generating sufficient revenue, revisit the Model phase so you can optimize it or fix what may be broken so you can increase your cash flow.

Harvest

The big financial shift in the Harvest phase is from how to *get* money to how to *return* money. I previously went into significant detail about different options for returning money to investors, so I'm not going to repeat that detail here. But I would ask you to consider this question: What is your financial goal for your start-up? If you want to create a sustainable enterprise, then you'll want to keep funding a long-term growth strategy. Some of you, however, will want to become serial start-up founders. You want to sell your business and return to phase one with a new company.

Be aware, though, that your "next start-up" only gets marginally easier. As someone who has gone through this process multiple times, I can assure you that it remains as hard as ever to have a great concept, nail the product, get traction, generate sufficient revenue, and so on. The long, cold winter of the J Curve trough is still a cold winter, though maybe not quite as long. In fact, it may even be harder because you've become soft; you succeeded, made it to Harvest, and sold your company for a substantial amount of money. You're comfortable, and that's not a great place to be as a founder. The J Curve winter is going to hit you (again) like a ton of bricks. You may be engaging in revisionist history or selective recall, saying to yourself, "Hey, it wasn't that bad." So let me remind you: Yes it was. It may have been exhilarating, but it was f$$$ing brutal, and the next one will be almost as brutal.

Think long and hard about cashing in, and consider staying with the wonderful company you've painstakingly built for another few years, or longer. You've worked incredibly hard to get to where you are—enjoy it and grow with it.

A FINANCIAL CHECKLIST

You're going to be grappling with thorny financial issues for the life of your start-up, and even though they may become less thorny in the Harvest phase, they still can be vexing even after your company is a success. To deal with early-, middle-, and late-phase issues effectively, some forethought is required, and that's what this checklist is designed to promote:

- Are you operating with a just-enough-resources mentality? Are you willing and able to run the company with the discipline and resourcefulness that scarcity fosters?

- Are you approaching multiple parties in your efforts to raise funds? Are you making sure that someone is minding the store while you're trying to generate funds? Are you targeting at least thirty different prospective investors?

- Have you considered bootstrapping as a financing option? Do you feel comfortable and able to use everything from mortgage equity to credit cards to your own cash to get the business up and running? Are you willing to make the tradeoff of keeping a day job in order to keep the cash flowing in exchange for the freedom from investor oversight?

- In Create, are you taking full advantage of the fact that it's a great time to raise money and may be the last time you can raise it for quite a while? Or are you thinking you need something tangible before they invest? Have you tried moving investors off the fence by generating interest in the start-up on multiple fronts and offering those who commit early a discount?

- In Release, are you eschewing such things as launch parties and hiring more staff in favor of conserving the cash you'll need to get through the long, cold winter?

- In Morph, are you dedicated to iterating until you find a product that clicks with customers? Are you moving as quickly and inexpensively as possible to reach this point?

- In Model, have you begun to target a list of prospective investors? Are you making initial contact with them? Or do you see your efforts as a way you can generate enough cash to put off the next fund-raising round?

- In Scale, are you exploring all your options (venture capital, banks, your own revenue) to fund your growth plan? Does it make more sense to grow at a moderate rate (requiring less capital) or bring in Sand Hill venture capital, get spendy, blow it out, and go big?

- In Harvest, have you made the perspective transition from getting money to returning it to investors? Do you really want to *ka-ching* this puppy and start over, or do you stay and continue to build the enterprise long term?

9

FAILURE:
MAKE IT YOUR FRIEND

There are two categories of failures with start-ups. First, the count-less series of mistakes, including judgment, product, features, peo-ple, markets, marketing, and sales, come at you like a river—they don't stop; they just keep coming. These types of day-to-day, tac-tical, or operational failures are perfectly natural, and they should not only be expected, but they should be embraced. You need to train yourself to become skilled at these types of failures. Second, there's the failure of the enterprise, which is to be avoided at all costs. It's important not to confuse these two different types of failure. A product failure, a people failure, or a feature failure is not a company failure unless you make it one.

If you're going to be in the start-up business, make operational failures your friend, while keeping in mind that enterprise failure is your most feared enemy. Your overarching goal is the success of the enterprise, but paradoxically, you only get there if you are good at dealing with operational failure. Therefore, prepare for the day-to-day failures and embrace them. I'm not suggesting you encourage failure. By all means, be tough as hell on mistakes, and if warranted, be tough on the people that make them. By suggesting you embrace failure, though, I want you to be ridiculously quick at spotting problems and equally efficacious at addressing and fixing those problems. I also want you to enjoy the challenges these situations offer.

Consider that the opposite of embracing failure is avoiding failure. There is no way in hell you can avoid failures in a start-up. It's just not going to happen. The failures are going to come at you relentlessly. They don't slow down through all the phases, with the exception of the Harvest stage, when life tends to get a lot more pleasant. If you are not prepared for failures and are not good at dealing with them, they will overrun you, and thereby imperil the enterprise. And again, you must *at all costs* avoid imperiling the enterprise. So embracing failure means that (1) you know failures are coming, (2) you are looking for them, (3) your extreme intellectual honesty allows you to perceive them early, while they are still relatively small and manageable, and (4) when the problem is in range you deal with it immediately and without hesitation.

If these different types of failure are confusing, let's clarify matters by differentiating our two types further. There are the day-to-day tactical and strategic failures, and then there is the catastrophic failure of the enterprise. In the latter instance, you have to shut the business down, investors lose their money and employees lose their jobs, and you have nothing to show for all your work except a negative reputation. So avoid this outcome at all costs. If in the end it must happen, execute it in a way that mitigates the damage—investors are repaid (in part or whole), employees leave satisfied, and your reputation remains intact. I'll show you how to do this later in the chapter.

What is common, indeed healthy, is where start-ups experience a number of discreet, limited failures involving products and business models, and those failures cause corrections that help morph them to a point where the product gains customer traction and the model starts generating a strong revenue stream. These failures provide valuable signals and market learnings for founders and their enterprises. Invaluable data is generated that can be analyzed and used to guide the creation of better products and models.

Given all this, I encourage founders to acknowledge and embrace these and other similar failures. Avoiding a declaration of failure is usually perilous. The worst damage is often done not by a particular failure but by not acknowledging it. Above all else, strive for the intellectual honesty that will allow you to identify failure quickly. You need it with yourself, and you need it from your cofounders and coworkers. Be aware that failure is tough to do properly in this great country of ours, because failure gets a bad rap here.

A CULTURAL PARADOX

In the US, and to varying degrees in other modernized countries, we appear to encourage taking risks in order to succeed greatly, but we discourage failure, which precludes us from taking risks. Let's look at the latter cultural imperative first.

We are a nation of competitors, and we play to win. If you recall ABC's *Wide World of Sports*, its introduction included film of athletes winning and losing events, accompanied by the voice-over narrator who intoned, "The thrill of victory, the agony of defeat." No one wanted to be the pictured ski jumper missing his takeoff and flailing his limbs as he cartwheeled through the air. Ouch. In the

US, winners are celebrated beyond all measure, and losers are often shamed, pitied, and forgotten.

It's difficult to reconcile this attitude toward failure with our seriously risk-loving culture. You can trace our risk-taking ethos back to the risk our ancestors took when they made a perilous ocean crossing. You can see it when our forefathers signed the Declaration of Independence, which was the initial business plan of the greatest start-up in history—the United States of America. If this plan didn't work out, the document's signatories would likely have been put to death; this was indeed bold risk taking.

So how do we resolve this conflict between celebrated risk and stigmatized failure? Start out by seeing it as a paradox rather than a conflict—success and risk are not incompatible. Rather, I would argue that they are inexorably linked. After all, risk always implies possible failure, and at the same time, the biggest start-up successes typically emerge from the riskiest ideas. It's pretty tough to achieve substantial success without taking equally sized risks. Fortunately, recognition of this fact is spreading, especially in major tech areas, such as San Francisco and surrounding environs, Seattle, Austin, and New York.

Another great paradox is that we tend to learn most from failure and least from success. For many people, success provides little data and stimulates scant reflection. It's rare indeed to do an autopsy on success. Failure, though, forces us to analyze all the data and learn what went wrong. Failure is painful, and it is that pain that eventually forces change. It forces you to take stock and consider other product, people, and business model options. When you're doing OK, you rarely consider these options. It's only the shock of failure that causes you to reassess, adapt, and find a better morphing path. So be open to it, be on the lookout for it, and don't ignore it when it arrives. Make failure your friend, and you will be a winner. Avoid it assiduously and you'll be a loser. By avoiding failure, you will make decisions too slowly, and time is the enemy of the start-up. Successful entrepreneurs embrace failure by learning the lessons, making the adjustments, and moving on.

TWO WAYS TO EXPERIENCE FAILURE

Your choice is fast or slow, and I'd advocate fast. Slow failures are agonizing, drawn-out struggles that always end badly. Here's a typical scenario. A founder ignores the facts that the market is communicating. He convinces himself that if he just has one more product feature, one more salesperson, one more marketing campaign, that everything will work out. So time passes, money flows out but doesn't come in, and eventually it is impossible to ignore the shrouded figure standing on his doorstep. Denials, rationalizations, and lack of intellectual honesty litter the road to slow failures.

This is opposed to failing fast—where you embrace the inevitable, own it, and deal with it as quickly as possible. You look at all the data and other feedback you're receiving, and if the product isn't working, the sooner you accept that fact, the sooner you can move on to something else. If you obsess about making the original idea work and rationalize that you're demonstrating stick-to-itiveness, you're simply denying yourself access to a better opportunity. Again, in order to master the fast fail, your best asset is intellectual honesty. Be honest with yourself, and require your team members to be equally and brutally honest. Self-delusion, or mass delusion of the team, will kill the start-up because it uses up too much time and money, depriving the start-up of the essential ability to switch directions.

From a J Curve perspective, failing fast is useful in every phase, but it is most critical in the Morph phase. It's impossible to ace the Morph phase without failing fast. It allows you to increase the speed of the iteration cycle, enabling you to try more ideas using less money. It also allows you to have more shots on goal, thereby increasing your odds of scoring a success. Since products and associated business models are only hypotheses at the start, and since most of them will be wrong, it only makes sense to embrace failing fast. Therefore, commit to failing fast. Your gut will tell you when the current product or business model is not going to work and iterations are not going to get you there. At that point, the proper thing to do is declare failure, which of course is the inverse of declaring victory. Say it out loud: "This is not working and I don't see any way it's going to, so let's talk about what we can do next to turn what we have into something that has a better shot at working." If you don't make your failure declaration loud and clear, your reticence will prevent you from morphing into something more successful.

When it comes to the enterprise's existence, however, failing fast should not apply. On the contrary, you need to have an unwavering commitment to the success of the company. Interestingly, it's the very commitment to the success of the enterprise that will help force you to deal with failures quickly and fail fast. For example, let's say you hired somebody who wasn't working out (which happens about 40 percent of the time). It needs to be your fear of enterprise failure and your commitment to its success that forces you to deal with that hiring failure immediately. If you don't act quickly, you are putting the enterprise at risk. An interviewer once asked my grandfather, George Love, who ran two of America's largest companies simultaneously, if he ever lost his temper at one of his employees. I expected him to acknowledge that he had and give some colorful examples, as I had known him to be a rather direct fellow. His response, however, surprised me as well as the interviewer. He said it never happened because the person would have been let go long before that became a possibility. He was so committed to the success of the enterprise that he wouldn't tolerate anyone who couldn't do their job well. They wouldn't be there long enough for him to get mad at them. That's dealing with failure quickly.

NEAR-DEATH EXPERIENCES

Virtually all start-ups will have a number of near-death experiences. Even when things get bad, though, you must be confident that somehow, you will survive. What gets you through those near-death experiences is commitment and perseverance, and you are not likely to make it through without a healthy dose of both. Oh yes, and being pigheaded and just refusing to fail also works fine (really).

With my first company, Inmark Development, we had so many near-death experiences that I lost count. As crisis followed calamity, my personal primary survival tool when the chips were down was plain old stubbornness. I was also mortified of the abyss that is enterprise failure. Just couldn't go there. And if I got shoved into that abyss, I shut my eyes, pretended I wasn't there, and scampered back to the ledge. It's worth referencing the qualities of commitment, determination, and perseverance, and those are certainly important and noble, but those terms seem overly regal in the context of a complete shit-storm. The fear, however, in those situations is quite palpable and visceral, and that specific fear can be a useful primary motivator. Thinking back, I recall each of the challenges with clarity and more than a bit of pain:

- Can't make payroll, check.

- Overdrawn at the bank, check.

- Maxed out the credit cards, check.

- Creditors calling, check.

- Employees bailing, check.

- Product struggling and taking forever to fix, check.

- Big make-or-break-the-company deals taking forever to close, check.

- Having no idea WTF to do to fix things, check.

- Haven't had a good night's sleep in a week, check.

- Looking at the shoeshine guy and being jealous that he at least has a steady income, check.

- Sleeping under the desk for days on end, check.

- Wondering how close I was to some sort of mental breakdown, check.

- Tears, check.

Be ready for all this, and more. Start-ups are very, very hard, and they are a contact sport. Start-ups can be the most rewarding of undertakings, but they can also just crush you at times. Elon Musk once said: "Starting a company is like eating glass and staring into the abyss." Take care of yourself and keep yourself healthy and in a position to handle large amounts of stress. This means engaging in regular exercise, maintaining a good diet, continuing great outside relationships, and so on. Keep communicating with your team; you need them more than ever during these tough times.

I managed to get through the near-death experiences at Inmark and other start-ups for the same reason lots of founders do: We're hopeless optimists, we love proving people wrong, we don't have the willingness or ability to work for other people, so if we can't make it, we'll starve. Someone once complimented me on having the courage to do a start-up, but it was a totally unearned compliment. I never thought of myself as courageous; I just liked to eat—and eat well!

IF IT REALLY, REALLY ISN'T WORKING OUT

Despite your commitment to the enterprise, there are times when you simply can't seem to make things work. You've failed fast and gone through a series of product iterations, you've tried different fixes, and even though you may have had some temporary successes, you're still not able to either break even or raise more money. You see the end of the runway coming and you're out of time and money. More importantly, you're out of ideas. When you've racked your brain and can't see anything else to try that is going to make a meaningful difference, then there does come a time when it's appropriate to throw in the towel. When you get to that point and you are quite sure that is where you're at, then you can still have a viable option where the outcome can be a net positive: executing a maneuver David and I refer to as a soft landing.

SOFT LANDINGS, HARD LANDINGS, AND YARD SALES

When you are ending a company, you can do it three different ways: the soft landing, the hard landing, or the yard sale. Which one you end up choosing has a major impact on the stakeholders—and your reputation. I'll describe the choices in reverse order of desirability.

The yard sale is characterized by a sudden and violent ending, like a train that is steaming along at full speed and slams into the side of a mountain. Nobody hit the brakes; in fact, nobody even blew the whistle. The passengers are sipping Ketel One martinis one moment, and the next moment, they are hurtling through the air. The yard sale implies that the company crashed, scattering its various parts all over the place, as in a yard sale. The stakeholders (employees, customers, creditors, investors, etc.) don't see it coming, and then boom, the company announces one day that it's all over, seemingly out of the blue. Typically, there is no money to pay the employees their last paycheck, creditors are stiffed, and customers are surprised and majorly inconvenienced. Investors not only lose all their money, but worse, they and the board of directors often have to spend substantial additional time and money to wind the company down properly. There are often lawsuits, threatened or real, and lots of upset people. Real damage is done. These types of situations are ugly, and people get hurt. I have seen a number of yard sales, but as a general rule, they should not happen. More to the point, allowing them to happen generally implies gross mismanagement by the management team and often the board. Everyone loses in a yard sale, so it is to be avoided at all costs. I'll repeat it again, do *not* end up in a yard sale.

The hard landing connotes a rough landing; employees lose their jobs, the investors lose their money, and the customer ends up without a product. But, in the end, the plane does land, and there is no catastrophic damage. If a hard landing is executed professionally, it's not a bad thing necessarily. The founder gives everyone a heads-up that there are serious issues, informs everyone as to what they are, sees the end coming, and avoids worse outcomes. Start-ups carry risks, and some fail despite the best efforts by management and employees to help them succeed. Most of the start-up ecosystem understands that, as long as they are dealt with professionally.

To execute a hard landing effectively, maintain regular communication with all the stakeholders and allow enough runway to land. Communication is so critical because people will understand and be understanding if they are given the facts. On the other hand, they hate being surprised. So when things are not going well, say so in your regular communications with your shareholders (which should be monthly or, at a minimum, once a quarter). In addition, make sure to give yourself enough time to execute a hard landing because it takes time and money to wind down a company. A properly executed hard landing is an acceptable outcome, in that if it is professionally done, it's neither bad nor good. Your reputation may take a minor ding, but nothing that can't be overcome with your next good idea and pitch. Past investors will still take your call, and they will appreciate the way you handled a difficult situation.

Your third option is a soft landing, in which you find a partner to merge with, or they buy the company and/or its assets. A soft landing ends with all or most of the stakeholders smiling, though well short of high fiving. No, the original dreams perhaps were not realized, but it's a decent outcome and importantly, much better than most were expecting. The key to a soft landing is to run the game plan in a disciplined and deliberate manner. In a soft landing, you package up whatever assets you have, including products, customers, employees, and relationships, and you pitch them to any and all interested parties. Here are the steps necessary for a proper soft landing:

1. Communicate with the investors and shareholders about the plan and ask for their support and assistance.

2. Make a list of all the potential partners who may be interested, and share the list with employees and shareholders

to see who might be able to provide an introduction. Make it an all-inclusive list, preferably with twenty-five to thirty prospects on it.

3. Make the pitch deck—exactly as you would if you were raising money. Focus on the people, the product, and the technology (if you have it) and how it might be a big win for the acquiring company.

4. Contact every company on the list methodically. Communicate exactly what is happening: You intend to find a partner within thirty days (or whatever appropriate time frame is but no more than sixty days). The time for playing games is over. Be direct, and don't be coy.

5. Set up a due diligence data room in the cloud (Dropbox or Google Drive), and have interested parties sign a nondisclosure agreement to access the data, which should include financials, contracts, pitch deck, and so on.

6. Run the process and choreograph it so that the interested parties are progressing roughly at the same rate.

7. Take the best deal. For investors, that could be a payout (up front or over time), a note, or an earn-out. The key here is to be flexible and commit to getting something done. Be a deal doer; don't be a deal talker.

My partner David is much better at executing these than I am, and it was he who developed this very effective formula. As investors or board members, we are aware that entrepreneurs usually have their confidence shaken at this point and may struggle to sell with confidence. For this reason, we point out that the company has far more assets than these entrepreneurs usually realize. Often, the acquiring company recognizes the value in not only buying the company's hard assets but its team; they can bring in great people who would otherwise be hard to get and cost a lot in recruiting fees. In fact, these situations are so common that they are now referred to as *aquihires*.

We have seen many successful soft landings executed by entrepreneurs we've backed, in which most of the employees retained their jobs with the new company, the product lived on, and the investors got some or all of their money back. There have even been several cases where, as investors, we made money. I know that David and I are extremely grateful when an entrepreneur executes a deft soft landing, and we are highly inclined to back those founders again down the road.

When David and I worked on GetawayZone early in our career, we made a lot of progress but ultimately realized that we couldn't generate or raise sufficient funds to scale the company. GetawayZone simplified the process of renting a vacation home, and we signed up a significant number of property managers and gained good traction on rentals, but we couldn't raise the money we needed to expand the business. So we began a search for potential partners, and made a prospect list. David either called or sent them a straightforward email pitching the company and the results we had achieved, as well as our financial requirements; he let them know that we intended to decide on a partner in thirty days. David was honest and no-nonsense in his approach, ensuring transparency. He also communicated clearly with all the investors, one of whom offered to provide an intro to another, better-funded start-up called VacationSpot. David began discussions with the VacationSpot management team and eventually settled on a deal where they acquired us for equity in the new venture.

David and most of our employees found good jobs with the new company. Shortly thereafter, VacationSpot was acquired again for equity by Expedia, and Expedia did well indeed over the next decade. In the end, the investors and the employees all benefited handsomely from this well-executed soft landing. It was successful because David ran the plan in a deliberate manner and chose a great partner with talented people and a bright future.

HIBERNATION

There is one alternative to pulling the plug on the company, and that is putting the company into hibernation mode. In hibernation, you cut expenses way, way back to something close to zero, or breakeven. You accept that progress will be limited going forward, but you expect there is a reasonable chance that time will offer some improvement in your situation. It's kind of like Texas hold 'em—you don't have a great hand but you want to stay in the game to see some more cards.

Hibernating a company, or a product, can make great sense under a specific set of circumstances. Specifically, if you believe that your company or product is a bit too early for the market and you want to wait it out. It is also an option if you need more time to think about it, or need more time to tinker with it to get it right. It's also appropriate if you have acquisition discussions going on but they are dragging out. The hibernation strategy doesn't work in competitive markets and doesn't work where there is the threat of rapid technical obsolescence, because in each of those cases, time will be working against you and you are unlikely to create more value than you presently have, especially at the reduced capacity of hibernation. If that is the case, you might as well try to realize whatever value you can immediately, however meager, because it's not likely to improve. But if you believe that time will be your friend and you are not threatened by competition or technology, hibernation can be a credible strategy, and I've seen it work on a number of occasions.

HOW EVEN SMART FOUNDERS CAN FAIL BADLY

I wish that most of the stories I know had happy endings and soft landings, but that isn't the case. It's not that founders fail poorly because they're naive or dumb or inexperienced (well, at least most aren't). It's simply that aversion to failure is hardwired into our culture, and this cultural influence affects the decisions founders make when things don't go according to plan. That's why even the smartest, savviest founders can make bad choices when things don't go well, as the following example illustrates. I've changed the names, but it's largely based on a true story. I know because my investment was a zero at the end, and I do tend to study those closely.

Eugene Cooper founded NewBonds Capital a number of years ago to cut out the traditional Wall Street bond traders and create an electronic exchange for bonds. Eugene, who had worked in the financial sector and was astute about this particular marketplace, had hit upon a good, plausible concept; the bond trading market was ripe for disruption. In other financial markets where things had remained the same for years, electronic alternatives had proven successful. Eugene was the first to introduce this more efficient approach to the bond market.

At the start, things looked promising. More than promising, actually, because Eugene raised a significant amount of money in the first round, $4 million. This was mistake #1: Raising too much capital on your first raise. Subsequent rounds raised that total to $20 million. Because so much money had been raised, Eugene decided to develop not one but two products simultaneously. This led to mistake #2: Developing two products at the same time. This showed a lack of focus and was only allowed to happen because there was an excess of capital. Compounding that error, Eugene decided to hire some expensive salespeople to penetrate the market, even though the product(s) were not yet finished. This is mistake #3: Trying to scale before you nail. The product was not fully baked, or, for that matter, even close, and the model was a long way from proven. Unfortunately, NewBonds Capital's first product never got off the ground because the partnering company got cold feet and backed out of the deal before the product could gain traction.

NewBonds' second product took a long time to develop because they never specced out a MVP, but rather allowed feature creep—yet another example of lack of discipline encouraged by too much money. The feature creep led to the creation of an overly complex product, which became so unwieldy that it became difficult to get it stable enough to release to the market. The CTO somehow was working on the second product and didn't have sufficient oversight. The CTO made a series of mistakes which went under the radar for a year because Eugene and his senior team were focused on the first product (with which the CTO wasn't involved). Eugene eventually replaced the CTO, but a lot of time was lost as they tried to come up with a new product.

When this product was finally released, it was too late for a number of reasons, including timing—the financial crisis and bond debacle in 2008 coincided with its launch. By 2010, the company had to fold with nothing to show for its efforts. Technically, it merged with another company, but it was a hard landing not a soft one because it was essentially a wipeout. Investors received nothing, and six years and $20 million were wasted. From a J Curve framework, whether he knew it or not, Eugene had never managed to move NewBonds past Morph (phase 3), where it was stuck. The company never achieved meaningful customer traction and market fit.

With hindsight, it's clear that Eugene made a series of bad decisions that resulted in his hard landing, including:

- **Raising too much money at the start.** As I've noted earlier, a surplus of initial funding creates a breeding ground for sloppy behavior. They tried to do too much (i.e., they tried to create two products simultaneously rather than focusing on the best one), they overhired and produced a high burn rate, and they didn't catch that the first CTO wasn't working out because there was too much going on.

- **Scaling before nailing the product or business model.** Eugene hired far too many salespeople too soon, in anticipation of becoming a much larger company rather than keeping overhead low and focusing on making a great product. This burned through a lot of money, not to mention time. It's perilous to get ahead of yourself on the J Curve.

- **Overengineering the original products rather than pursuing an MVP.** The company would have been much better off spending the time up front to define and build an MVP with a limited feature set and using that to get customer traction. Then, it would have had a customer base that would have given it the product feedback it needed to decide what new features would be important. Instead, the product suffered from feature creep and arrived bloated.

So failure can cause even a smart, experienced entrepreneur like Eugene to make the wrong moves. The good news is that you can protect yourself from making these mistakes and learn to make the right moves when things go wrong.

HONESTY IS THE BEST POLICY

When you experience various failures in your start-up—and let me assure you, you will—then you have to resolve to be honest with yourself. Brutally honest. This means that when the data emerges, you must try to figure out what the customer and the market are telling you. The best founders have the capacity to push aside their egos, their biases, and everything else and view the feedback for what it is. As much as the feedback may hurt, they don't try to rationalize what they're hearing or, even worse, deny it.

Instead, they take an honest look at the situation and respond with blinding speed. They don't waste time with lots of meetings to interpret the data. They don't look for second and third opinions from outside consultants to confirm what they already know. Instead, they and their team are quick to kill their products or features when they need killing; and they're just as quick to iterate and come up with a new and improved idea that has a better chance of gaining customer traction. These founders are a joy to work with; they understand what to do when failure happens and how to quickly move beyond it. They know that the quickest way to success is to embrace the failures and move quickly through them.

Contrary to what many people believe, it's not that great entrepreneurs succeed because of their special intuition (though that helps), it's that they are brutally honest with themselves and their team, and they read the data and react immediately, creating another iteration in record time. When brutal, intellectual honesty is combined with resourcefulness and relentless execution, your odds of success skyrocket. Those that have them both, either innately or because they personally embrace and commit to them, get to product/market fit nirvana quickly. The long, cold winter of the J Curve seems more like a ski vacation.

This is as opposed to founders who, upon hearing the bad news about their product, prevaricate and procrastinate. They refuse to acknowledge the elephant in the room, and they don't want to hear the brutal truth that the first release of their product actually just sucks. They retreat to *we need one more feature* land. Even when they are forced to confront the ugly reality, they throw their hands up as if there is nothing that can be done. They take things personally, and they are hapless and passive. They allow the world to work on them as opposed to imposing their will on the world. They say things like, "I'm not sure if *x* is the issue" and "Maybe we should give it more time and see what happens." At best, they move in slow motion; at worst, they become paralyzed. Even though the writing is on the wall, they don't let it sink in. Instead, they act as if time will be a failed product's friend, and it's anything but. In fact, with start-ups, time is more precious and scarce than money.

While time is not your friend, honesty is. Intellectual honesty allows you to get more out of a fixed quantity of time. Make a commitment to being intellectually honest with yourself and your team. It will help you identify the inevitable failures and move through them quickly.

"KNOW WHEN TO HOLD 'EM, KNOW WHEN TO FOLD 'EM"

This quote was taken from the song "The Gambler" by Kenny Rogers, and start-ups and poker carry a number of similarities. This hold 'em or fold 'em is worth thinking about when you're confronted with difficult situations. I think there are two situations where it's entirely appropriate, indeed advisable, to call it quits. The first is when your health or that of your family is suffering; you can't have a healthy start-up unless you are healthy. Nothing is more important than your health. The second is if you've run out of ideas on what to do next. You've brainstormed, you've iterated, you've morphed, and you still aren't there. You've tried everything, and now you are out of ideas. Time to call the game, shut down the company, take a break, and start again on another venture when you are up for it.

For instance, as committed as you may be to the enterprise's survival, this commitment can be taken to an extreme where you may be doing both you and your company more harm than good. William Norsk was the smart and talented founder of a start-up, and I was coaching him, because I had a substantial investment in his company and it was enduring some hard knocks. Foremost among them, his company had been the victim of a nasty lawsuit, a lawsuit that William eventually won, but it had taken a toll on him and really dinged his confidence. In addition, his primary market had slowed down considerably due to a nasty economy and had become intensely competitive; the companies that were doing well possessed exceptional operational excellence, a quality William was lacking. I had put far more than my normal allocation into the company and, sometimes against my better judgment, I had still continued to write checks when needed. But I had hit my limit and nobody else was willing to step up. William had not taken a vacation in years, and he was struggling to make a sufficient income to feed and maintain his family.

Nonetheless, William wanted to keep going, to sustain his vision for the company. I was aware of the tremendous stress he was under and the toll it was taking on him professionally and personally. So I had to do something unusual; I used all my powers of persuasion to convince him that the best thing to do was give up. I didn't see any way to win, and I was concerned about my friend's health and general well-being. To William's credit, he not only took this advice but executed a nearly flawless soft landing. He managed to pay off all his debts and had a good plan to return at least a portion of his investors' capital. I was incredibly grateful for this, as I was planning on having to come up with another $50,000 to properly shut the company down. After taking some time off, William has regrouped and is already working on his next start-up, which he generously gave me a piece of.

Of course, as I am fond of saying, the world is rarely black or white. It's a gray and complex situation when you're stuck in start-up limbo—you haven't exactly failed, but you haven't exactly succeeded either. I call these companies the walking wounded, and usually about one third of my venture investments end up this way. The start-up isn't losing much or any money, so it keeps limping along. At the same time, nothing a founder does seems to help it take off. Selling it is a possibility, but it's one most founders reject because they won't get much for it. Plus, founders still believe that it might take off, and they don't want to jettison it prematurely.

And it might take off, but probably not unless something substantial changes. In these situations, figure out a catalyst to help it skyrocket. If your investors are on board and your team agrees—and if you're not burned out, like William—then look for a spark, or better yet, a bonfire. I'm not in favor of tweaks in these situations because they don't change the fundamentals. Rather, you need to manufacture something substantial enough to jolt the company. My favorite thing to do in these situations, if the founder is amenable, is to bring in a very senior person—a new CEO or somebody strong enough to be an equal or near-equal partner with the CEO. A fresh perspective and additional brainpower often provides exactly what the company needs to get it out of the doldrums.

THE FAILURE CHECKLIST

The goal is to fail fast in the short run and to succeed in the long run. Few sustainable enterprises exist that lack a history of failure, so don't let the stigma of failure stand in your way. Here are some questions that will help you embrace and capitalize on the inevitable mistakes and defeats your start-up encounters:

- Are you operating with a clear definition of failure? Do you recognize the value of small feature, product, or business model failures versus the failure of the enterprise?

- Have you reconciled the seeming conflict between failure and risk? Are you able to view them as a paradox that exists in all successful start-ups?

- Are you willing to fail fast? Can you avoid the time-consuming excuses, analysis, and serial meetings that delay the inevitable? Are you able to let go of your original idea, learn from the feedback, adapt, and move on to the next, better one?

- To determine if you can keep the enterprise going, have you tested fixes and found them untenable? Have you solicited feedback from a diversity of sources?

- With the prospect of enterprise failure looming, are you trying to create a soft landing? Or are you postponing the inevitable and dithering away with fixes that have no chance of working, thereby increasing the chances of a hard landing or yard sale?

- Are you making decisions that can lead to the failure of the enterprise, such as raising too much money at its inception, not concentrating your efforts in creating an MVP, scaling before nailing the product or the business model?

- Are you and your team brutally, intellectually honest about the feedback and data you're receiving from customers and the marketplace? Or are you spinning it to yourself and your team in ways that cause you to postpone the inevitable?

- Are you under such an enormous amount of stress that it no longer makes sense for you to push forward? Are you concerned about your health in any way? Aside from normal flare-ups, is your spouse in this with you and hanging tough?

- Is it fair to characterize your start-up as being in limbo—neither succeeding nor failing—and are you willing to do something major that catalyzes positive movement, such as bringing in a new CEO or high-level partner?

10

THE PERSONAL SIDE OF THE START-UP LIFE

More so than in the corporate world, success in start-ups depends as much on who you are as what you do. As a founder, you're going on a personal journey, and if you haven't been on it before, you'll grow immensely. You'll learn a wide range of lessons as you move through the J Curve phases—lessons about everything from resiliency to humility to creativity.

At the same time, prepare yourself to be tested. Nobody arrives at start-ups with what it takes. Even the greats have stumbled. Steve Jobs got booted from Apple. PayPal fired Elon Musk. Speaking of Musk, in Ashlee Vance's biography of him, he talks about low points at two of his companies, SpaceX and Tesla: "I was just getting pistol-whipped . . . There were always all these negative articles about Tesla, and the stories about SpaceX's third failure . . . I didn't think we would overcome it. I thought things were probably f****** doomed."

I don't quote this passage to scare you, but to prepare you. You're going to run into criticism and crises and all sorts of situations you've never experienced before, so expect the unexpected. To help you get ready, let me begin by addressing the biggest personal challenge you're likely to face and how to deal with it effectively.

CRISIS POINTS

Start-ups are like hospital emergency rooms—you're going to be faced with desperate situations and catastrophes on a regular basis. One day, you realize you can't make payroll or your top salesperson suddenly quits. Suppliers are clamoring to get paid and you can't raise additional funds. In these circumstances, your biggest challenge is not to bail. If it's any comfort, most start-ups go through these crisis points and emerge whole. Things get rough, but founders with grit and determination tough it out (again, with the caveat of "until it affects your personal health").

Admittedly, when you're enmeshed in a crisis, you may lack a positive perspective. In fact, you may echo Musk's earlier quoted words about being f****** doomed. But even if you feel this way, recognize that your ability to hunker down and persevere is what will see you through the crisis.

I've noticed a disturbing trend among start-up founders in the last year or two, which I blame on the current frothy environment: People fail to stay the course. At the first or second crisis, they bail. It's one of the reasons, I've greatly slowed down new investments. In the current tech bubble, start-ups are trendy, and they attract some participants who are drawn to the seemingly hip trend rather than those who possess the deep drive and determination to make it past the setbacks and obstacles on what is likely to be a seven- to ten-year epic journey. In a blog on his site, David Cohen, founder of leading Internet start-up accelerator Techstars, writes that "Start-ups are 'quitting' when the first year doesn't go as planned . . . start-ups are hard . . . It takes persistence and dedication in almost every case if you hope to be successful."

So how do you weather a crisis successfully? Here are three traits that serve founders well when things are darkest:

- **Passionate dedication to your mission.** Elon Musk, for instance, is dedicated to saving our planet by ending our reliance on fossil fuels (Tesla, Solar City); his vision also encompasses colonizing other planets to avoid the possible extinction of earth (SpaceX). This may not be a typical corporate mission, but Musk is absolutely committed to it, and this is what drives him through crises. Musk spent the entire fortune he had accumulated from PayPal to save Tesla and SpaceX at a critical period when the consensus assumed they would fail. Just at the point when everything was collapsing and it looked he was "f***** doomed," he doubled down and went all-in.

- **Fear.** Founders are motivated by the fear they might lose their investors' money or let down their employees and customers. Scared of being embarrassed or failing to live up to others' expectations, they work hard and innovatively to escape that fate. Fear is a powerful motivator, and it's one that start-up founders draw upon. It's not the most pleasant of motivations, but it's usually there to some extent, and it's effective. Fear is a fickle mistress and a tricky one to dance with: One moment it's an exhilarating tango partner; the next minute it's a sloppy drunk in need of therapy. Accept fear as a motivator, but don't let it get the best of you.

- **Perseverance.** The most successful start-up founders may all have wildly different personalities, but just about all of them are determined, especially in their refusal to give up. They are committed, and they persevere. And no matter how successful they might have been in the past, they retain that chip-on-their-shoulder attitude that communicates, "Screw everyone who thinks I'm going to fail; I *will* prove them wrong." They don't throw in the towel even when things get bad, hating the idea of others saying, "I told you so." By refusing to give up, they are often able to survive the worst days when all logic says stop and are ready when opportunities finally present themselves.

A PERSONAL LOOK AT THE PHASES

Each phase of the J Curve presents different personal challenges to different people. Because every founder brings his or her own mix of personal traits and skills to the start-up, every founder is going to experience the challenges in his or her own way. One individual may find the Morph phase the most challenging from a personal standpoint, while another person may struggle with the Scale phase.

If this is your first time running a start-up, you will struggle in at least one of the phases and probably more. If you're a start-up veteran, you will still struggle, but you probably have a better idea of your weaknesses and how to manage around them. You also have an idea of what to do when the usual hiccups come. You won't become a basket case when you find yourself struggling to meet payroll because you've learned you have various options to deal with this situation—or you've become savvy enough about start-up financing to avoid a payroll crisis. You probably have also figured out that it helps a lot to acquire skills you're lacking—either learning them yourself or bringing in partners who possess these skills.

Be aware of how each phase will challenge you. Knowing the ways a given phase affects people will prepare you for what's to come. Being conscious of the traits you need to exhibit to get through a phase successfully—and the emotional traps founders may fall into—can help you navigate the phase better.

Create

In this first phase, you need to connect with your passion and mission. What will sustain you through this phase—and help you make it through all the phases—links what you care about deeply with the product you're creating. Be aware that I'm not referring to possessing a passion to make a lot of money or to become fabulously rich and famous. There's nothing wrong with wanting to become wealthy—who doesn't want to make a lot of money from a start-up—but by itself, this is usually an insufficient mission. Whether your passion is to create products that help facilitate social media communication or promote physical health or provide better ways to shop for cars, it's something you're driven to do. When things get tough—and they always do—you can draw from your deeply held belief in what you're doing and keep going.

This passion is communicated to investors—they are impressed not only by your knowledge but by your commitment to your start-up product. If these investors are smart, they know that you're the one likely to stay the course and work overtime to make the start-up successful.

The Create phase draws on a variety of skills and traits. As the phase name implies, you need to be creative, matching your passion to a product. You also must be disciplined and committed, focusing on keeping things simple and in the MVP zone.

Release

This is where high expectations run smack dab into disappointing realities. You've dreamed about the world embracing your product for months or even years, and once you make it available, you're greeted with moderate sales at best and indifference or negativity at worst. Even moderate sales can be devastating, since they are a dream crusher.

Don't become despondent if your product doesn't take off in its original state. It's rare for the original product to be the one that shoots the start-up into the stratosphere. It's fine to be disappointed, but don't become enervated and unable to rebound from negative feedback.

Similarly, you need to develop a thick skin so you can assess market reaction to your product objectively and astutely. If you become defensive, you'll end up denying the feedback.

Morph

This phase, like the first phase, tests your creativity. The task is to iterate, shift, and evolve your initial product until it resonates with customers. Creativity is an underrated skill for start-up founders, but it's one that is crucial, since it helps you imagine how your product can match with what the customer wants.

As you consider iterations, be brutally honest with yourself so you hear what the marketplace is telling you; and in turn, level with your team about what you're hearing. Intellectual honesty is what saves you here because it allows you to react faster and more accurately.

Model

Here founders need to be sticklers for detail, especially as it relates to costs. If you're a big-picture thinker who can't stand to get bogged down in numbers and operational details, you're going to struggle in this phase. It's time to monetize the business, and one of the key requirements is nailing down every cost you have and cutting them to the bone (while maintaining quality).

SpaceX's competitors spent $100,000 on an industrial radio for their rockets, while SpaceX figured out how to use off-the-shelf parts to create a similar radio for $5,000. It took an engineer a year to figure that out, but combined with many similar efforts at SpaceX collectively, it allowed them to produce a rocket for less than half of the prevailing prices. Founders need to be sticklers for detail during this phase, and if they can't do it, they need to bring in partners who can.

Scale

In many ways, this is the most personally challenging phase because it's such a change from the previous phases. Because the skills required are so different—you have to get the money, put processes in place, and find specialists and delegate to them—you may struggle with the transition to Scale. The company will change significantly, and many individuals will struggle with that change.

By struggle, I mean you and others may resist the demands of this phase and continue to try and do everything yourself. From a company perspective, what's required in the Scale phase is a switch from generalists to specialists. You can no longer free range and bop from one functional area to another. The functional areas need to become siloed, otherwise there will be chaos. If you are the CEO, your job at this point is to start delegating to the professionals. You know you are failing at this if it becomes obvious that you are becoming a bottleneck. Your inclination will be to maintain the status quo, a huge mistake personally and professionally. Few if any CEOs possess all the skills necessary to handle the expanding functional responsibilities. You're inviting huge stress and possible burnout if you refuse to bring in experts and delegate.

Flexibility and leadership are two traits that serve people well during this phase. Because the company's and people's roles are changing during Scale, agility is necessary to accommodate these changes. Being agile is a challenge to founders with cowboy mentalities; they resent having to submit an expense report to get reimbursed. To avoid chaos in an ever-expanding organization, leadership is essential. You may miss the old days when your small team functioned without titles or a chain of command, but if you persist in running the company as a co-op, you're going to be running it into the ground. Accept your leadership role, and while it's possible that you can use the old small-team approach on occasion, more structure is necessary in this phase.

Finally, you're going to require all the energy you can muster. To say that scaling is exhausting is an understatement. Be prepared for a whirlwind of activity—people to hire, sales to make, trips to take, presentations to give, production to oversee. You may well find yourself exhausted from lack of sleep and gaining twenty pounds from being on the road. So take care of yourself. And more to the point, take care of the growing business by delegating. Theoretically, you've hired specialists who know more about their functions than you. Let them do their jobs. If they are not up to the task, then get somebody who is. Don't make the mistake of trying to make all the decisions like you did when the company was smaller; you're asking for a nervous breakdown at best and a heart attack at worst. You don't want people frustrated because you've become a bottleneck for decision making; and you can't have the new, rather expensive professionals twiddling their thumbs while you try to decide. Delegating allows you to focus your energy on key matters that you're best suited to handle.

Harvest

Wisdom will help you move through this phase successfully. Wisdom, of course, isn't something that you can simply click your heels and acquire. It comes only with knowledge tempered by experience. Wisdom will help you avoid doing anything dumb or rash, a common trap during Harvest. You've built a wonderful company; don't screw it up.

My grandfather, George Love, was a highly successful and prominent business leader in the fifties and sixties. One day he was having lunch at a golf club he had built and where he was president, and an acquaintance stopped by and introduced a friend he had in tow.

"Nice to meet you, Mr. Love," the friend said. "Tell me, what do you do?"

My grandfather was not shy about listing his accomplishments, and he began to tick them off: "Well, I'm chairman and CEO of Consolidated Coal, chairman of Chrysler, on the board of General Electric ..."

He was just getting warmed up when this friend cut him off and said, "Well, George, that all sounds terribly important. Make sure you don't f*** it up!"

We all laughed when my grandfather used to tell that story, and the message was a good one. Once you've built up a great enterprise, stay humble and don't do dumb things. To avoid acting in unwise ways during Harvest, create a formal and informal network of advisers. On the formal side, create a board of directors if you don't already have one. On the informal side, gather trusted and savvy people outside of your business who can guide your efforts. When he arrived in Silicon Valley, Facebook's Mark Zuckerberg reached out to leaders in the area to give him the lay of the land, including Steve Jobs. Some people were quick to dismiss this East Coast interloper in the hoodie when he arrived, but they soon learned that he was connecting with people who had been there, done that. By talking with and getting advice from other entrepreneurs who had built large companies, he was able to avoid many common pitfalls. Facebook board member Don Graham said, "Jobs meant an enormous amount to the education of Mark. Mark will talk about that until the cows come home." (See http://www.businessinsider .com/steve-jobs-mark-zuckerberg-walter-isaacson-fortune-brain-storm-2012-7.) You, too, would do well to find mentors who can help you navigate tough situations.

Wisdom arrives through your own experiences as well as through your personal network of people you admire. By supplementing all this with a lot of reading and other learning, you can increase your personal store of wisdom and feel confident that you won't screw things up in this last phase.

THE AGE FACTOR

Start-ups are a bit like playing football; the game tends to favor the young. But I don't in any way want to discourage people who are as old as I (or older) from pursuing their start-up dreams. Speaking as someone who has his AARP card, I do want to point out some of the challenges my generation faces, so you will be able to address them and deal with them rather than having them deal with you. One striking paradox is that wisdom serves you wonderfully in the Harvest phase, but it may trip you up in the first few phases. Knowing too much can impede the type of instinctive running and cutting that is ideal for the initial phases of the J Curve—instinctive moves foster the creativity that is key in these early phases. Naïveté will kill you in Scale and Harvest, but it is a big asset in the previous four phases. Therefore, your age may have a bearing on how the start-up experience affects you on a personal level.

If you're a younger founder—say in your twenties or thirties— you possess certain personal advantages that may offset your lack of experiences and concomitant wisdom. For instance, you may be in a better position to take risks than an older entrepreneur with more financial responsibilities. If you're single, don't have children, and have relatively few significant debts, then you're more likely to tolerate the pressure that comes in the J Curve's dark days. You also know that you have plenty of time to recover if things do go to hell in a handbasket. It's a bigger challenge for an older individual with a family and all sorts of other responsibilities (mortgages on the house, college education bills, etc.) to take the risks and maintain the commitment necessary.

As I've noted, there's no substitute for wisdom, so even though you may find the risk and stress more problematic, you are sufficiently savvy and can make astute decisions even when you're under pressure. If you're an older entrepreneur, however, be aware of the following three personal challenges. These are generalizations, but if you are aware of them, then I think you'll be in a good position to overcome them:

- **Brain plasticity.** It's tough to make the mental leap of envisioning how a product or service that others dismiss or see as wacky can become a winner. As we age, we tend to not be as nimble in our thinking as when we were younger—we know too much and can see all the potential problems. When we're young, we aren't burdened with all that knowledge, our minds tend to be a bit more adventurous, and we are able to see myriad possibilities.

- **Lack of naïveté.** The older we get, the more hard-boiled and cynical we are tempted to become. As I've noted earlier, it helps to be sufficiently naive about what's possible. When you see how daunting the path ahead is, the less eager you will be to set foot on it. I'm fifty-five as of this writing, and I can tell you that it gets tougher for me each year in this regard. I have to remind myself to be open to possibilities and not be a naysayer, since all my experience informs me of what could go wrong. I find this struggle to stay relevant to be my biggest challenge. I need to force myself to listen, to pick up on new trends, and then look at them and ask, "How can this be big?" rather than dismiss them out of hand. I also have to remind myself that, for most new products, I'm not the target customer.

- **Stamina.** It takes a great deal of energy, focus, and strength to succeed as a start-up founder. Going through the six phases of the J Curve can take a lot out of you. When you're young, you're generally in better physical shape; you've got energy to burn. When you're older, you may not appreciate working twenty-four hours a day, seven days a week or the humbling process of asking for investment funds.

DO YOU HAVE THE TRAITS IT TAKES?

Regardless of your age, certain personal qualities will facilitate your start-up success. Certainly start-up founders' personalities vary widely—some are outgoing and loquacious, others are introverted and reticent. You can't change your personality to conform to the ideal founder, but you can be aware of the qualities that increase the likelihood of success. The odds are that you'll possess one or two of these traits and perhaps have some natural ability in others.

Work to develop these traits to the maximum, and if you're lacking some, find partners or other people who can add these characteristics to your team:

Resourcefulness

As Paul Graham wrote in an essay published on his site (http://www.paulgraham.com/relres.html) titled *Relentlessly Resourceful*, he explains that this is the critical quality for a start-up founder (versus being hapless). Based on my own experience, I concur with Graham. The world is divided into those who impose their will on the world versus those who too easily accept what the world imposes on them. As my kids are tired of hearing me say, there are Ameri*cans* and Ameri*cants*. The former are problem solvers and take the initiative. They bristle over discussing the problem and prefer action. If something is not working, they tinker until they can jerry-rig a solution. If they're trying to get through to someone and the admin runs interference, they find a way around the admin—either calling before the admin arrives for work or sweet talking the admin into putting them through. As an investor, I've found that resourceful founders tend to see problems, solve them, and then report them (to me) in that order. By contrast, Ameri*cants* tend to ignore problems when confronted with them; they finger point, complain, talk, wonder if they really exist, and finally try to get somebody else to solve them.

Resilience

Since so much of a start-up involves failing at things, you need the ability to bounce back. If you are trying to create something new, different, and unfamiliar, you may be ignored or mocked; you certainly will have a lot of doors shut in your face. If you have an innate ability to take rejection, learn from it, and then push forward, you'll be able to tolerate the naysayers without it dampening your energy or enthusiasm.

Comfort with the Unknown

Some people need all the facts and figures before they act; they require certitude about everything from trends to markets before they launch a product. These individuals don't do well in start-ups because they can't tolerate all the unknowns that are part of the experience. Until the Harvest phase, you're operating with the ground shifting under your feet continuously. Being open to the unknown is the best way to capitalize on the opportunities and solve the problems that pop up regularly.

Perseverance

I've noted this quality previously because it's so important in a start-up environment. I'm not being hyperbolic when I state that the average person would give up on the start-up before phase 2 or 3 based on their tolerance for setbacks, unwanted surprises, and crises. You have to be committed to make the start-up successful, and at times, you must demonstrate an obstinate, even pig-headed determination to make your business successful. My partner David likes to quote a close mutual friend who says, "Perseverance through adversity leads to success."

Sales ability

This is a hugely helpful quality, since start-up founders are constantly trying to:

- raise money,

- get customers,

- entice good people to join the company,

- generate media attention or stories or blogs, and

- convince the team to listen and believe.

I'm a mediocre salesperson, and that's been a limiting factor. I've backed entrepreneurs who couldn't sell and then been forced to step in and try to help secure the next round of funding, which has been unfortunate, since I would struggle to sell a cold Gatorade to a man in the desert. I've been fortunate to align myself with people who are much better at selling than I am. I've also witnessed master salespeople (I call them promoters) who are able to obtain far more money, talent, and media attention than their product deserves. It's not fair, but it's reality.

Finally, you may have noticed that one quality I haven't included in this list is intelligence. Fortunately, you don't have to be a genius to be a successful start-up founder. Sure, being smart can help you in a lot of ways, and Stanford, Berkeley, MIT, and Harvard have produced an outsized number of entrepreneurs that went on to raise venture capital, but given a choice between a resourceful, passionate, and persevering entrepreneur and one who has an off-the-charts IQ,

I'd choose the former every time (http://www.entrepreneur.com /article/236912). If you're dedicated to your venture, your passion will drive you to care more, know more, and think more about what you're doing than your competitors.

ARE YOU A MISSIONARY OR A MERCENARY?

This question goes to the heart of why you're in the start-up business. Mercenaries do what they do for money. Missionaries do what they do because they believe deeply in their company's mission and are committed to how their product or company might change the world for the better. They tend to focus on producing products or services that have a perceived social utility. Steve Jobs was the classic missionary, hell-bent on changing the world and refusing to let anything stand in his way. Less well-known but possessing the same missionary zeal are a number of founders David and I have worked with, including Sara Sutton Fell of FlexJobs, who is bringing the opportunity of flexible and remote employment to millions of people; Sam Shank of Hotel-Tonight, who is changing the way we book hotels (making it a less expensive, more spontaneous process); and Hein Van Wyk of Share-Faith who is helping churches modernize and stay relevant.

As an investor, I prefer to give money to missionaries in part because they tend to have significantly larger outcomes. Sometimes, they can be a bit more difficult to work with because who they are is tied intimately to their work mission. But they also are committed and relentless. Even better, they tend to recruit other missionaries who commit to their cause. While missionaries have a higher burnout rate than mercenaries, this negative is more than made up by their loyalty and desire to work for meaning over money—the latter is a way for them to keep score.

It's not that mercenaries can't be successful start-up founders; they are, and I've worked with some of them and watched how their emphasis on metrics helps them make the numbers. They can be superb operationally, and in fact, many of the S&P 500 CEOs are mercenaries. But unlike missionaries, the goals of mercenaries tend to be personal rather than tied to the product or company. For instance, some mercenary founders might say something like the following in their initial presentation: "I think we can build this up and sell it for $30 million." I take these statements as bad signs, since it usually means they aren't as driven or committed to their products and customers as they are the numbers. If I hear that comment, I don't invest. Mercenaries may achieve their goals, but they often aren't as ambitious and long term as missionaries. They tend to cash out early, which kills my returns as an investor.

Understand that the line between missionaries and mercenaries isn't hard and fixed. Start-ups change people. Some people start out as mercenaries but become missionaries as they move through the start-up phases. Also, most people have a mix of missionary and mercenary qualities; it's unusual to find someone who is 100 percent pure.

WHAT'S YOUR WHY?

Whether you are a missionary or a mercenary raises the fundamental question of why you are embarking on your start-up journey. My friend and former Navy SEAL Commander, Mark Divine, boils it down to this question: "What is your why?" Mark was ten years active on SEAL teams and ten years in the reserves. He then started a company called SEALFit that helps train prospective SEALs as well as civilian adventurers to test themselves. SEALFit's ultimate test is called Kokoro Camp, and it's a fifty-hour, nonstop crucible training event modeled after the Navy SEAL Hell Week. That is fifty hours straight of hard-core mental and physical exertion, with no sleep. Less than 50 percent of the class will finish the ordeal. At some point during the camp, Mark asks students to state their *why* for attending the camp. Mark can often get a strong sense of whether they will successfully complete the training based on their answers. Here are some typical responses to the why question:

- "I am here to prove that I am tough enough to be a Navy SEAL." (This is *not* a strong why, and these guys often fail.)

- "I want to prove to my two daughters that I am strong and will always be there for them." (Lottery winner! This woman crushed it.)

- "I want to meet my true self and push through my self-imposed limitations." (This is a solid why.)

- "My father enrolled me and I want to prove to him I am worthy of this program." (This is another fail.)

According to Mark, "The key point here is that when the dark night of the soul moment comes, when your mind and body say they are done, and if the student can't dig into a deep reservoir of inspiration to continue, then they won't. The why is the tap to that reservoir, and having a powerful why that is intrinsic and deeply meaningful is required to stay the course through the most trying times." The missionaries know their why, and it is something bigger than themselves. The mercenaries may not know their why because it's all about them; they don't have a larger purpose.

Navy SEAL Hell Week training is particularly relevant with respect to pushing through as opposed to quitting. The primary objective of Hell Week for the Navy is to smoke out the quitters. They need the quitters gone quickly for two reasons. The first is a simple investment issue: They don't want to put time and money into training those who are going to eventually quit, since it's a bad allocation of resources. Second, and perhaps more importantly, it's a matter of life or death. The one thing that SEALs cannot have happen under any circumstances is for a team member to quit in the middle of a firefight. If that happens, there is a good chance that somebody may get killed. Needless to say there is nothing touchy-feely about Hell Week, no kumbaya sessions; rather, the drill instructors are purposely trying to get you to quit. You better have a good why or you are going to be crawling over to ring the bell, thereby ringing out and joining the more than 75 percent who quit.

While start-ups may not be life or death literally, they are exactly that figuratively. In start-ups, you will be tested in many ways, and more than once, you'll probably consider quitting. The strength of your why will determine whether you have the determination to push through the adversity to success. Be conscious about your own missionary and mercenary tendencies. Ask yourself what type of product or business will trigger your missionary impulse and help you build a start-up around it. If you choose something that you are passionate about and through which you have a chance to make a significant impact, you're not only more likely to be successful financially, but you're also more likely to have a fulfilling and meaningful start-up experience. Therefore:

- pursue what really turns you on, what you're super passionate about;

- focus on products and services that are fun and have some social utility;

- find people with whom you really enjoy working;

- realize that you're on a journey;

- embrace the unknown; and

- refuse to give up, unless you are out of ideas or your health is jeopardized.

A PERSONAL CHECKLIST

Do you have the right stuff to be a start-up founder? Typically, people think about this *stuff* as meaning that they possess a great product idea or the financial backing to launch the product. But it's more than that. The most successful founders possess specific traits and especially a powerful drive to succeed no matter what obstacles are thrown in their way. You don't have to possess every desirable characteristic, but you should be aware of them and either cultivate them or align yourself with a partner who does.

To assess your own personal capacity to succeed as a founder, think about how you'd respond to the following questions:

- If your start-up ran into a major problem—one of your top people quits suddenly or your funding dries up—do you think you'd have the grit and gumption necessary to keep moving forward? Are you sufficiently dedicated to your mission, fearful of failure, and obstinate that you won't let anything deter you from achieving your start-up objective?

- In the Create phase, have you connected your product or company to your mission?

- In the Release phase, have you steeled yourself for marketplace indifference and negative feedback? Are you prepared to move forward even after having your dreams dashed by customers?

- In the Morph phase, are you capable of being brutally honest with yourself and your team, no matter how negative the feedback might be?

- In the Model phase, are you willing to dig into the details to figure out how best to monetize the business?

- In the Scale phase, are you capable of not doing everything yourself and finding and delegating to specialists?

- In the Harvest phase, are you willing and able to tap into formal and informal networks in order to avoid rash and potentially destructive behavior?

- Are you aware of how your age or wisdom affects your ability to run a start-up successfully? Do you recognize that if you're relatively young, you probably are more willing to take risks but lack the wisdom experience confers? And if you're older, your challenges will include less stamina and ability to make imaginative leaps of faith about products or the business?

- Of the five key traits for start-up founders— resourcefulness, resilience, comfort with the unknown, perseverance, sales ability—which ones are your strengths and which ones do you lack? Are you willing to bring in other people to supplement the areas where you're weak?

- Are you a missionary or a mercenary? If you're more of the latter or a mix of the two, can you make the effort necessary to connect your product or business to your driving passion?

11

LEVERAGING THE J CURVE IN LARGE ORGANIZATIONS

As you probably know, large organizations often struggle to remain innovative. If you were to measure innovation on a per-person or per-dollar basis, it looks pretty bad for large corporations. Governments and the military suffer from the same issues as large organizations. Breakthrough innovation requires a certain amount of chaos, and large corporations tend to be orderly places. As much as the leaders of these corporations might want to foster disruptive innovation, their policies, structure, and processes often mitigate against it. Employees may be perfectly capable of embracing failure and creating two, three, or more versions of an initial product, but the organization doesn't like failure; its formal and informal rewards system is built around success. As a result, people aren't motivated to take risks, to iterate, to be wildly creative. Just as troubling, the people charged with fostering innovation are often individuals researching the category and various related matters, and as such, they're removed from direct interactions with and feedback from customers. Thus, they base their innovations on researched data rather than product experiences.

But what does this have to do with you? You're in the start-up business, not the corporate arena. True, but the odds are good that you may transition into that world one way or another. Let's look at those transition points and how the J Curve can make your stay in that sphere a highly productive one.

WORKING LARGE: THE JOURNEY FROM START-UP TO CORPORATE

Your start-up may intersect with the larger, corporate world in a variety of ways, but let's focus on the following common possibilities:

- You sell your start-up to a large organization in the Harvest phase and as a newly minted corporate citizen, want to drive growth through innovative products in this larger enterprise.

- You've moved from the Scale to Harvest phases and become sufficiently large that it's more difficult to create and sell innovative products inside the company than when you were small; you've grown to the point that you're essentially a small corporation rather than a large start-up.

- You are a corporate (or government or military) employee but want to find a way to make your slow-moving, risk-averse, innovatively challenged organization function more like a start-up (or at least the group or team of which you're a member).

In these and other situations, you need a tool to facilitate product innovation in an environment that may not be conducive to innovation. Size alone is a deterrent, as is bureaucracy and phlegmatic processes that take forever to approve new initiatives. The good news is that the J Curve can be exactly the tool you need to overcome the corporate obstacles that stand in your path.

Fundamentally, the J Curve is about getting from an initial idea to a useful product or service in the most efficient manner possible, utilizing limited resources in the shortest amount of time. The secret of the J Curve is embracing the unknown and using flexibility to make the most of the opportunities that present themselves. To understand why these attributes are so important in corporate settings, let's take a quick look at why innovation is such a struggle in large organizations.

Consider that many of the blockbuster drugs marketed by pharmaceutical companies come to them via acquisitions rather than through their R&D pipeline. Consider, too, that large tech companies such as Microsoft and Yahoo struggled to produce game-changing innovations on their own as they became large enterprises and had to rely on incremental improvements and upgrades to existing products. Even worse, their hubris about doing all their own inventing caused them to resist acquiring innovative technologies.

The challenge for large organizations is allowing the chaotic process of invention free reign, and that's something many organizations find difficult to do. As I noted earlier, innovation emerges from chaos, and chaos isn't something that management relishes. That's unfortunate, since radical innovation, especially, is rarely a planned process. To facilitate product morphing, organizations need to be open to every option, to accommodate failures, and to test product ideas that seem to come out of left field.

Even start-ups struggle with the chaos of innovation as they move from Model to Scale. Specialists who operate in the silos of their expertise don't always think beyond their functional boundaries. It's the generalists who are frequently the masters of innovation and are able to draw from a diversity of ideas and sources to come up with something new. Large organizations, of course, are filled with specialists in silos, adding another obstacle beyond the cultural aversion to chaos.

Fortunately, the J Curve can provide you with a way to stay as innovative as ever whether you're a corporate employee or a corporate ally. And equally fortunate, larger companies do actually have some very meaningful advantages that can be leveraged. Let's look at how the J Curve does so through the lens of each phase.

PHASING IN INNOVATION

From a J Curve perspective, corporations do have an advantage in the Model, Scale, and Harvest phases. They're practiced at the tasks required in these phases, so they can often move through them efficiently and effectively. It's the first three phases that give big companies the most trouble, so the trick is to leverage the company's generalists during these initial phases, protect them from the organization, and allow them to engage in rapid prototyping, focusing on MVPs and producing rapid iterations to gain significant customer adoption. Then, once this is achieved, the company can involve the rest of the organization in the last three phases.

More specifically, let's look at this process on a phase-by-phase basis:

Create

The good news is that large organizations are already tuned into market signals and are receiving feedback from customers, so they possess the type of information that can fuel the creation of innovative products. The bad news is that their structure and culture will hamper their efforts.

Therefore, the first thing you should do is form a small, protected team. They need to be protected because they will engage in activities that violate stated and unstated corporate policies, including creating MVPs instead of fully baked products, moving forward without a solid product plan, and morphing—changing direction quickly. The general corporation is not going to like that nor should they. A large corporation cannot function with a start-up's speed, agility, and lack of structure. So there needs to be a real distinction between the two so folks don't get confused. Steve Jobs protected his start-up-like groups by keeping them small and keeping them secret. If the rest of the company doesn't know about it, they can't get in the way. As Steve was well aware, early ideas are very fragile. They can't survive if the corporate heavyweights are dumping on them.

Here is how Jony Ives, Apple's brilliant designer, recalls it: "Steve used to say to me—and he used to say this a lot—'Hey Jony, here's a dopey idea.' And sometimes they were . . . But sometimes, they took the air from the room and they left us both completely silent. Bold, crazy, magnificent ideas. Or quiet simple ones, which in their subtlety, their detail, they were utterly profound . . . he treated the process of creativity with a rare and a wonderful reverence . . . while ideas ultimately can be so powerful, they begin as fragile, barely formed thoughts, so easily missed, so easily compromised, so easily just squished."

So somehow, the large corporation needs to create an environment where the sprouts of new ideas don't get crushed, and that is not easy. It doesn't happen without commitment from the top.

The start-up group should have their own funding (just enough to create a product) and the ability to operate independently. In fact, it's ideal if they can work in offices separate from the corporation. Again ideally, this team has its own leader or CEO who is different from the parent company's CEO. Essentially, the corporation acts as the board of directors of this new team or venture, providing guidance and assistance but not interfering in daily decision making.

One potential advantage for corporations in this Create phase is that they don't have to be first to market with a product; they possess the resources to identify the mistakes made by other companies as well as the customer needs a given product isn't meeting. For instance, Steve Jobs and Apple weren't the first in the market for portable music players; they entered when the market was flooded with many such devices, mostly in the MP3 format. What Jobs saw was: (1) they were not very good; (2) they did not offer a seamless way to purchase, manage, and play music; (3) Apple's size and brand would allow them to put together a deal with the music companies; and (4) Apple was already selling computers that would be the necessary link to the music, positioning the company to deliver an end-to-end solution. In other words, Apple did well in Create because it was *already* a substantial corporation. Its size and market penetration allowed it to pressure the record companies into collaborating to offer its music in a single-song purchase format. This would have been much harder for a raw start-up—perhaps impossible. Jobs also knew that he lacked critical technology, so he was able to leverage Apple's corporate finances to buy the technology and expertise that would be needed to cobble the full solution together. Again, it was easier and faster to get money from the corporate coffers than raising it from investors.

Release

Corporations usually have superior supply chains and are adept at distributing products with speed and effectiveness. A new venture can take advantage of this distribution power (assuming the corporation has the same or a similar target market). Many times, however, big companies take forever to release products, often in an understandable attempt to protect the brand. The phlegmatic pace can drive start-up founders nuts, so if you find yourself dealing with the slow-moving release pace of a large organization, here are three shortcut options you could use individually or combined:

Call the product *beta*. Once you communicate to your corporate colleagues and potential customers that this isn't a fully baked product, you help overcome much caution and slow decision making that comes when a company is releasing what they believe to be the product in its final form. Obviously, this tactic is more difficult to implement if your product is an automobile versus software. Still, corporate bosses recognize there are many early adopters out there who will put up with all sorts of product glitches to be the first to try a cutting-edge product. Given these early adopters, the company feels confident their brand is protected.

Another option is to set up the new product in a different division or subsidiary with a different brand name. Again, this protects the corporate brand and assuages concerns about an imperfect product tarnishing the brand. If the product is successful, it can be rolled up into the parent brand. If it's not successful or is marginal, it can exist as a spinoff.

You can also commit to iterating quickly after the initial product release. By communicating this strategy to the corporation, you help them understand that your goal is essentially rapid test marketing, and that you intend to move from version 1.0 to 3.0 or 4.0 with great speed. Microsoft has been proficient at using this method, introducing 1.0 versions that are famously imperfect but immediately improving them with rapid subsequent releases and usually getting it right by the third version. By listening to feedback about each version and then improving the product based on that feedback, they can create a marketable product relatively quickly—and without earning the enmity of impatient corporate leaders wondering why the initial version was so flawed.

Morph

This phase presents the biggest challenge for large companies; they are not usually nimble enough to change direction once, let alone twice or three times. Admitting failure quickly, coming up with a promising morph, then repeating the process in rapid succession can be a major challenge in cultures where admitting mistakes is taboo.

As we've seen, however, the J Curve provides a compelling case for failing, listening to feedback, and trying again. When organizations understand the Morph phase and how it can lead to a bigger success than sticking with the first product idea, they may recognize that this process is critical to innovation. At the very least, the new venture requires a CEO or another powerful sponsor to provide a given team with the freedom to fail. This can be done in four ways:

- You report directly to the CEO or another senior leader who is supportive of innovation, start-ups, and the J Curve process.

- You're physically separated from the rest of the corporation, operating out of a different office or location and thereby insulating you from the failure-averse culture.

- Your project operates under the cloak of darkness; you're a secret or semi-secret team whose invisibility allows you to try, fail, and morph three or four times without repercussions.

- You are operating in a corporate culture that is forgiving of honest mistakes.

Companies are generally OK and maybe even good at making small iterative changes, but they are typically bad at morphing. They lack flexibility, hate failure and avoid it, and they despise the unknown (it doesn't budget out too well). Large companies pride themselves on predictability, a trait strongly encouraged by Wall Street. So for a large company to encourage morphing, they need to recognize their tendencies and create a plan to mitigate or eliminate them when it comes to an entrepreneurial team.

Model

In this phase, large organizations have a significant advantage because they have an infrastructure in place, including supplier relationships, payment systems, advertising strategies, and so on. This is a particularly important advantage if the new product has a substantially similar model. Even if doesn't, though, the existing relationships and infrastructure is a big advantage. If nothing else, it's easier for a large company to get the attention of suppliers and vendors than it is for an independent start-up that has no established name and limited resources.

A founder who has grown his company by leaps and bounds may revisit the model, but more often, he will iterate it and grow its possibilities. GoPro started primarily as a specialized camera company but eventually became an "action camera and media" company.

Scale

When you're the size of, or partnering with, a larger enterprise, you gain the advantage of speed in this phase; you can leverage existing people, processes, and distribution to expand internally and externally at a fast pace.

Scaling is where large corporations really shine, and they have huge advantages over a start-up because they possess three primary ingredients: people, process, and money:

- **People**: Large corporations already have specialists in place that operate at Scale with great effectiveness. They stick to and are expert in their domains, and they know how to communicate and operate with the other operational silos of a corporation (marketing, sales, engineering, finance, etc.).

- **Process**: They have in place a production process, the distribution, the financial accounting, the customer service, and so on that will operate at Scale in a reasonably smooth manner. These processes are critical when you are operating on multiple fronts; without them, chaos is the result.

- **Money**: Corporations, presumably, have a source of cash flow that CEOs can direct wherever they want. While the CEO has a board and shareholders to answer to, she still has great sway and discretion, and importantly, the company doesn't grind to a halt when she focuses her attention on fund-raising. So having this supply of cash flow is a huge advantage, because real money is usually required for scaling.

Harvest

Unlike start-ups, corporations operate in a continuous Harvest mode. So they have real experience with this phase and can deal with the opportunities and major financial questions without missing a beat. They are either already a public company, or they are an established private company with an existing policy on what to do with the cash flow. They already have established expectations with their investors and other core constituents. They will distribute, invest in additional growth or products, or use the cash to pursue acquisitions. Large companies are so used to the Harvest stage, they can do it blindfolded.

ASSESSING THE CORPORATE EXPERIENCE

As someone who believes strongly in the start-up culture and its value to the business world and the larger society, I am the last person to tell you that you should run out and join a corporation or even that you should establish an alliance with one. At the same time, I also believe in keeping my options open and would advise you to do the same. It's also a question of what fits best with your personality; some do best in the chaos of a start-up and others thrive in the more structured environment of a larger corporation. A time may come when an opportunity presents itself to join a larger company and, if you think it's a good one, then you should at least consider it.

Sometimes, corporations provide a short-term respite from the uncertainty and financial struggles of the start-up life. There's something to be said for a steady paycheck, great resources, and benefit plans. And as large organizations attempt to be more like start-ups—more innovative, more accepting of failure, more willing to accept a diversity of personalities and operating styles—you might find it to be a rewarding experience.

I've found that start-up founders are drawn into the corporate world via three motivating factors:

- **The opportunity to fully realize the promise of a product by blowing it out into the world.** Large corporations offer *insta-scaling* because they have the three magic ingredients needed for scaling: money, people, and process. You can put a great product into a corporation, and suddenly, it's everywhere. Large corporations may not be adept at innovation, but they are masterful at Scale; they can blow a product out much faster than can a start-up.

- **The chance to gain corporate experience.** Many start-up founders are business greenhorns and need some seasoning. Corporations provide it. So when you exit the corporation, you will be in a better position to be a successful start-up founder because you possess better contacts, managerial, and organizational skills and scaling abilities.

- **The opportunity to help an acquiring company obtain maximum value from your start-up.** You may have a financial incentive to help the corporation that buys you succeed, such as an earn out. You want the acquiring corporation to be successful with their acquisition. It's important to your reputation that you deliver on what you represented during the negotiations. Acquiring companies usually struggle initially to run a business they have acquired, so you can facilitate the transition if you are involved and engaged. Make sure they are successful with their purchase; it's the right thing to do, and it's important for your reputation.

Finally, be aware that the start-up founder's relationship with a corporation usually falls into one of two categories: being acquired or forming some type of partnership.

In the former instance, right after the purchase, the corporation moves into the Scale phase, which is often a good thing. If you've nailed Morph and Model, then a corporation's infusion of resources plus their strong infrastructure can move your start-up into the major leagues. Corporate types assume that the start-up people and culture will be absorbed into their own—that they'll become good corporate citizens—and that usually doesn't happen, at least not right away. As a result, tensions can run high and create frustrations. It's OK to protect your people and products so the company doesn't accidently kill what it acquired. It's a balancing act.

In the latter situation, you've established some sort of alliance with a corporation. To be honest, I'm not a big fan of a lot of partnerships because I've seen so many result in dashed hopes and wasted time. The primary problem with partnerships is that both companies have different agendas. The start-up often has unrealistic expectations of what the corporation is going to do. They delude themselves and think they are going to influence or modify the priorities of the company. That never happens. Start-up founders often seduce themselves into thinking that the big, partnering company will solve all their problems, and they rarely do.

The exception to my "be wary of partnerships" rule is when a large corporation is providing a limited, specific, well-defined service for the start-up, and when it's easy for the start-up to get out of the relationship if things go south. At LoveToKnow, we have a number of partnerships with advertising networks that generally work out well. Expectations are not too high, everyone knows it's a relationship of convenience, and both sides recognize that they need to deliver or they'll get dropped like a stone. The relationship is friendly but professional and focused on the specifics of the business. There are no big dinners with bro hugs and fine wine and grand prognostications about how together we are going to conquer the world. Those just don't work. When the relationship is clearly defined and limited in scope, then the partnership can work for both parties.

A CORPORATE APPLICATIONS CHECKLIST

Whether you've become a corporate employee or are working with a large organization while still a start-up founder, recognize that factors exist affecting your success that are different from when you were operating as a small, independent entity. These factors can be both positive and negative, but it's more likely that they'll be positive if you are aware of them and are sufficiently agile to shift your approach to take advantage of them.

To help you do so, consider these questions:

- Is the large organization with which you're associated hamstrung by a slow-moving approval process, bureaucracy, and difficulty accepting any type of failure? Are there ways you might incorporate aspects of the

J Curve to facilitate the speed, flexibility, and innovation that characterize the best start-ups?

- In the Create phase, can you form a small team that is insulated and protected from the pressures, bureaucracy, and procedures that can make it difficult to come up with truly innovative products?

- In the Release phase, are you able to speed up the process of getting a product out there by either creating a beta product, releasing it under a different brand name, or committing to come out with different versions of it quickly—or doing all three?

- In the Morph phase, are you able to overcome the innate organizational resistance to making major, wholesale product changes by having your effort fly under the corporate radar or by operating as a company within a company and not subject to the typical corporate oversight?

- In the Model phase, are you able to capitalize on the large organization's infrastructure that the company may already have in place?

- In the Scale phase, are you taking advantage of the organization's people, process, and money resources? Can you leverage the existing customer lists and marketing infrastructure?

- In the Harvest phase, are you drawing on the corporation's extensive experience with using excess cash for investing, new products, growth, and so on?

- Do you possess a clear goal for your corporate relationship? Do you hope that it will help you acquire knowledge and skills that you can put to use for future start-ups? Do you believe corporate resources will help bring your product to a much larger market?

12

MOVING FORWARD

As of this writing, start-ups are the stars of the business world. Given the success of Uber, Snapchat, WhatsApp, and many other tech-based companies and their rapid rise from ideas to billion dollar *unicorn* enterprises, entrepreneurs are more apt to launch an app than open a shoe store or build a better widget. More to the point, the start-up model holds tremendous appeal because of speed, technology, and attractiveness to investors.

But things change, and as quickly as people hop on bandwagons, they hop off. If you're going to do a start-up, you had better be serious about it and have a very long-term time horizon. Being an entrepreneur is a career, not a gig. The average start-up takes seven to ten years from conception to liquidity, so you need to prepare for a long haul. If your first start-up doesn't make it for whatever reason, you need to be ready to reload for the next one—and the next one. Even in the best of times, this is no business for dilettantes.

Commitment is crucial, and the J Curve is going to work best for founders who are willing to make a commitment. I cannot overemphasize this belief, and as I look at the current environment and the opportunities and challenges ahead, I think you'll better understand this point of emphasis. Consider, then, the bubble that currently envelops the start-up world, and when it's likely to burst.

BUBBLES COME AND GO; ENTREPRENEURS STAY THE COURSE

When should you start your start-up? Is the best time now (fall 2015), when it seems like everyone is into start-ups and investors are receptive to all sorts of tech concepts? Or should you take a cue from the financial markets and buy when everyone else is selling, waiting until the bubble bursts and avoiding the start-up company clutter that exists in the current boom times?

In fact, the right answer is none of the above. It's tough to time both the stock and start-up markets, so in most instances, you shouldn't worry about the perfect moment to launch since you're going to experience a roller coaster ride no matter what things are like when you begin. Start-ups and technology tend to follow a boom or bust cycle, and it's best to be prepared for both. Right now, it feels like we're at the top of the boom, and invariably, this period will be followed by a rough patch in which money dries up, start-ups struggle, and a shakeout occurs. But in the end, it really doesn't matter, because after the bust another up cycle will arrive. The long-term trend is inexorably up.

While all industries are cyclical in nature, the cycle is intensified in the tech field. Since moving to Silicon Valley more than twenty years ago, I've seen a number of up-and-down periods. When I first arrived here in 1991, it was a down period; the local economy was doing poorly, a large percentage of Silicon Valley office buildings were in bankruptcy, and a *Time* magazine's story titled "How Grey is My Valley: The land of high tech suffers a wrenching mid-life crisis" referred to Silicon Valley as *Gloomy Gulch*. The article noted, "Gone are the days when development spreads like brush fire across the region and upstart businesses leaped from garages to the Fortune 500." In fact, the next nine years proved to be one of the greatest growth spurts for technology in our history, culminating in one of the largest bubbles to ever happen in America. Then, the Internet bubble popped in early 2000 and the tech market had a spectacular crash; I remember hosting a dinner party in 2002, and when I looked around the table at our ten guests, I realized that all of them were out of work. From that bottom, a fast run-up to 2007–2008 took place, when the macroeconomic events related to the financial crises overwhelmed every part of the economy, including tech, and we had the financial meltdown. From the 2009 bottom, another great run-up occurred to get us to the lofty and precarious levels where we are now. There are two primary problems with the current market: (1) too many start-ups have been funded and are dependent on future funding that doesn't exist, and (2) there are 150 so-called unicorns, whose last funding round valued the company at $1 billion or more where only a small fraction of those will (in my opinion) maintain or surpass that valuation in five years.

So besides being mentally prepared for alternating up-and-down periods of varying lengths, the best strategy for when things are going great is to prepare for the inevitable downswing: Raise as much cash as possible, try not to spend it, and get to positive cash flow ASAP. I realize that this advice isn't always easy to follow, but at the very least, focus on creating that positive cash flow. While you can't control the larger economic environment, you have the most control over your own company. I always think of cash-flow positive as nirvana, because if you are cash-flow positive, you control your own destiny. By contrast, if you are losing money, someone else will eventually control your destiny for you.

Be aware, too, that what you're doing is important, not just to you, your family, your employees, and your investors, but to the larger world. Innovation in every sector is critical, and start-ups are where innovation happens. Even more important is that start-ups that are innovating new technologies will be at the forefront of the economy and society as a whole. As Ray Kurzweil points out in his book, The Age of Spiritual Machines, the pace of change increases over time. Not much happened in the first few thousand years of our time on earth; there has been a lot more change in the last thousand years than in the thousand before that. In the last one hundred years, the rate of change has accelerated beyond anything in the past, and even more transformative change has taken place in the last twenty years.

Technology drives this change, so start-ups have a critical role to play in the coming years. Despite the roller coaster ride ahead, the prospects for tech start-ups are better than ever before, since they will comprise an increasingly large percentage of a metamorphosing world and its economies.

EMERGING OPPORTUNITIES

In the coming years, start-ups will shine in a variety of fields, especially those where innovation is in demand. For instance, health care is a field crying out for innovative solutions to a range of complex problems, and myriad opportunities exist for start-ups. If you're considering starting a business in this field, though, you should proceed with caution. In health care and in other sectors as well, governmental regulations can interfere with a start-up's ability to innovate.

In health care, the need for innovative solutions to rising costs is critical, but regulatory friction often prevents disruptive innovators from creating game-changing products. Onerous regulations pose problems for start-ups because they don't have the resources necessary to understand and navigate around them. In addition, overly regulated industries discourage investors from putting money into start-ups in these industries. On top of that, start-up founders recognize that even if they were able to launch a product that the market embraced, corporate lobbyists might influence regulatory bodies in ways that would put start-ups at a competitive disadvantage.

Government represents a big opportunity for implementation of the J Curve and support of its process. The paradox is that if government really wanted to encourage innovation in health care and other fields, they would step back and allow a free market to flourish and the J Curve to work its magic. Further, they would review existing regulations and eliminate the superfluous and counterproductive ones. HIPPA regulation, for instance, was designed to ensure medical records privacy. While it's well-intended, HIPPA has introduced massive frictional costs into the system with relatively little impact on the problem it was intended to solve. As a result, every health care start-up has to deal with the HIPPA hurdle, and many are so discouraged by the costs of clearing that hurdle that they often look to other fields that aren't as tightly regulated.

Unfortunately, government often acts with an arrogant belief in single, permanent solutions to problems rather than embracing the uncertain reality exemplified by the J Curve. But laws, like business plans, are rarely perfect and are famous for spawning unintended consequences, often serious negative ones. The Dodd-Frank legislation, for example, had the unintended effect of shutting down the mortgage market for the middle class—even Ben Bernanke, the former Chairman of the Federal Reserve, was denied a home loan. We'd all be better off if all laws came with sunset provisions in which lawmakers had to review their efficacy at one-, three-, and five-year intervals and modify the laws based on monitoring the real-world impact of a given law. In this way, they would pass and then change regulations in the same way the J Curve mandates Release, Morph, Model, and Scale.

Government-funded research grants are another area that would benefit greatly from embracing the realities of the J Curve. The current format of research grants is that the researcher submits a grant proposal, and if it gets funded, the researcher must adhere precisely to the submitted proposal. So, even if it becomes obvious that the original hypothesis was incorrect, the researcher must play it out, spend the balance of the research money, and then publish the results. On the surface, this appears to make total sense. After all, the researcher is simply doing what she said she would do. But in the context of the J Curve, it is a horribly inefficient way to spend research money. The J Curve predicts that the original plan almost never works and that the big discoveries are made only after taking an early look at the data and then morphing into a substantially different plan. A better, far more efficient system of research grants would build in all of the flexibility needed to leverage the power of the J Curve.

Artificial intelligence is a promising field, even if it's been an investment dud for the past forty years. Perhaps it's because sufficient computing power is available to make it a reality, but new products such as IBM Watson are gaining real traction and making a difference. Robotics is another field that is growing out off the factory floors and into the home; indeed, R2D2 will be here shortly. Drones are proliferating so quickly that the government is struggling to keep up. Virtual reality is a virtual certainty. Genetic bioengineering is just a matter of time. Even though the current state of the products in these fields is rough, in a few short years, these emerging industries and others will meaningfully impact our lives. I encourage you to force yourself to understand these trends and to immerse your imagination in the possible opportunities that they might offer.

But the truth is that often we don't see the next big thing coming. It arrives like the black swan that Nassim Taleb so brilliantly writes about: "First, it is an outlier, as it lies outside the realm of regular expectations, because nothing in the past can convincingly point to its possibility. Second, it carries an extreme 'impact.' Third, in spite of its outlier status, human nature makes us concoct explanations for its occurrence after the fact, making it explainable and predictable." If you are adept at the J Curve and embracing the unknown, then you'll be comfortably unsurprised at the surprising and in a great position to capitalize on it.

WHAT YOU MIGHT LOVE TO KNOW

Throughout this book, I've related a variety of stories about start-ups that I hope have motivated you as well as helped you identify potential mistakes and traps. I've saved one story for last, in part because I wanted to give you a firm grounding in the J Curve's phases before telling it, and in part because it's a good story to keep in mind as you move forward.

I started LoveToKnow during 2003 in the wake of the Internet bubble bursting apart. The hedge fund I had been running was underwater, my income dropped almost to zero, and I had a mortgage and my family to take care of. On top of that, my wine selections had migrated to the bargain bin, and that alone was putting me in a grumpy mood. I had that most primal of motivations: my family and I needed to eat! The good news was that I had an idea for a new business. I was 90 percent mercenary and 10 percent missionary. Perhaps more accurately, my mission was to make at least enough money to cover my family expenses.

But this mission changed as my start-up evolved. This change is instructive, and it's best viewed through the six phases of the J Curve:

- **Create**. My original business plan revolved around constructing a website that curated the best ten websites for every major information category on the Internet. By sifting through the search results and handpicking the truly great sites, we would be superior to any search engine. At the time, it seemed like a breakthrough concept, although in retrospect, there was nothing magical about it. It seems really silly in retrospect, but I swore people to secrecy because I was so certain this would be a huge success right out of the gate. Though I had little money to launch the start-up, I managed to assemble a great team of part-time employees to get the company off the ground. I found a wonderful developer in India via a Craigslist ad. I also found a great designer through my brother-in-law. I added a small editorial team, and we were ready to roll.

- **Release**. We did a fair job of getting the product released. As is always the case, it took longer than we expected or desired. But lack of funds is a great motivator and an underappreciated asset. So I didn't fall prey to the get-ting-it-perfect trap. Rather, we just got the damn thing out—we had to! And, even the initial release looked pretty darn good, and we released it with great optimism. But it's fair to say that the initial product hit the market with a thud. It was a bit like a tree falling in the wilderness. Nobody heard it, and nobody cared.

- **Morph**. While the site attracted some users, it didn't achieve the success we had anticipated and was not going to be a sustainable business. We listened to the data to see what direction we should move in. Based on feedback, the original search directory concept was the wrong direction. However, we had started a side project—information about how to choose engagement rings of all things—that, accord-ing to our web analytics, was generating outsized traffic. The market was telling us that the top ten idea was OK but not great. The specialized information about engagement rings, however, showed more promise, so we began moving our resources to support this project. We also added some specialized editorial team members more suited to this new morphed approach. We began testing other categories to offer similar types of information and advice such as wed-dings, babies, and dogs. Some of these early team members ended up forming our core team that continues today.

- **Model**. The business model that emerged at this point was clear: Spend money to create super high-quality articles that give people the information they are looking for, publish in a pleasing magazine-level format, sell advertising, then rein-vest cash flow.

- **Scale**. Once we nailed the model, we branched out and eventually had over fifty channels. Hiring great people along the way, we turned the LoveToKnow name into one of the web's most trusted information brands where people would be confident they would get the information they were looking for.

- **Harvest**. Our goal was never to sell the company, so we built it into a sustainable enterprise with good cash flow characteristics. As a result, we also made a number of tactical and opportunistic acquisitions, including YourDictionary.com, which launched us into the online dictionary business, and GolfLink, which got us into the sports category. We continue to search for top digital media acquisitions to strengthen an already strong brand. Somewhere along the journey, I fell in love with digital publishing and realized that I derived immense joy from working with the incredibly talented LoveToKnow team. I consider myself fortunate indeed to work with such an amazing group of professionals.

I learned a number of lessons from transitioning my start-up through the phases of the J Curve, and these lessons may help you on your start-up journey:

- **Be flexible and open-minded about where your start-up takes you**. I started as a mercenary and ended up a missionary. From simply wanting (actually needing) to make money, I segued into an evangelist for digital media. I liked my original business product, but I loved how that product morphed. Rather than become fixated on the original concept, I followed the feedback, was flexible, and was able to move the company in new and much more profitable directions, eventually becoming one of the largest digital media companies in the country.

- **Hire great people who can do the job better than you can.** As the business grew, I brought in amazingly talented individuals who possessed expertise I lacked. And I recognized that the best thing I could do was let them do their jobs and focus on helping them get through roadblocks.

- **Acquire financial discipline.** Most start-ups begin with tight budgets, and this is a good thing. Like people who grew up in the Depression, founders who make it through the long, cold winter of the J Curve learn how to spend strategically and save wherever possible. If you have financial discipline, you're much more likely to survive the tough patches that every business encounters.

Looking back, I find it a bit astonishing that we followed the J Curve precisely even before I had mapped out this model. With hindsight, I realize that we were fortunate to adhere to the phases as closely as we did; it probably saved us from disaster more times than I care to count. Still, it would have been nice from a confidence standpoint to know we were following a normal and viable model. As I pointed out in this book's introduction, it would have been nice to have had this book thirty years ago; it would have saved me a lot of pain and suffering. But then again, I wouldn't want to change (much) of the journey, because the journey is the whole point. The destination is the journey, and the journey is the destination. And what a journey it has been.

So I offer you the J Curve in the hope that it makes your entrepreneurial journey that much easier and that much more successful. I trust that this model will serve as the roadmap described in the first chapter, giving you a sense of where you are at different points in the journey, and that subsequent chapters offer guidance on the best things to do (as well as what not to do) at each of these points. Finally, and perhaps most importantly, I've written this book to inspire you to take the journey and stick with it. I've shared stories of my own journey as well as those of other start-up founders to help you learn from the challenges all of us have faced.

While the J Curve may be revolutionary in terms of describing an underlying process that people and groups go through to bring about something new, I believe its six phases have always existed and will always exist. It describes a fundamental process of human beings working to solve problems and create a better life. When you have a vision and seek to implement that vision, you are on the J Curve, whether you realize it or not. I think it's been there since the caveman developed the spear, and it's still there today as Elon Musk develops interplanetary travel at SpaceX.

As you go through your journey, keep the J Curve handy. Invariably, you're going to reach a place when you feel confused and lost, and that's when the J Curve can provide help and hope. It can provide the reassurance and direction that are invaluable at many different points on your start-up path; it will give you the confidence to persevere and reach your dreams. The world needs you to pursue your dreams, however crazy, since that's what keeps the world moving forward. As Steve Jobs once said, "Stay hungry, stay foolish." Good luck. I'll be rooting for you.

ACKNOWLEDGMENTS

I've been blessed in my life to be positively influenced by such a wide variety of family and friends. First, of course, is my amazing wife Harriet, who has always put up with the vagaries of my entrepreneurial adventures for the past twenty-five years. She has celebrated with me when times were good and calmed me when times were tough. She has given me the strength to go do crazy things (like writing this book) and sometimes many crazy things at once. I can't imagine doing hard stuff without her loving support, and fortunately I haven't had to! My incredible three children, Annabel, Peter, and Kirk, are an inspiration to me in thousands of ways, one of which is a reminder to try to leave the world a little better place than I found it.

My venture partner for the past twenty years or so has been David Hehman, and a better partner I could not have. He is incredibly steady, smart, has unimpeachable integrity, and is a lot of fun to work with on a daily basis. I've tried a couple of "solo acts" where I invested, mostly unsuccessfully, without David, and those experiences have only reinforced how lucky I am to have him as a business partner and close friend.

My parents have always been incredibly supportive of my various ventures. My mom's tireless energy and enthusiasm has always been an inspiration and a source of strength. My dad taught by example that even though you may be successful in business, as he certainly was, don't forget to live and enjoy life. Everyone enjoyed his presence and we all miss him. My father also taught me a lot by taking me around to various business meetings. Those meetings showed me firsthand how to conduct and comport oneself in business environments and are probably the reason I have always been comfortable in business settings. I often think how, as a parent, we can teach our kids so much by showing them what we do and how we do it. They aren't going to learn that at school. If I am driving the kids somewhere, I don't hesitate to put business calls on the speakerphone so they can hear how business is conducted (so be forewarned)!

I've been fortunate to have four incredible siblings—Marion, George, Jane, and Victoria—who have put up with my whacky ideas and notions of how the world works. I know they have my back, and I'm thankful for the warm and close relationships we all have together.

Both of my grandfathers, George Vaughn and George Love, were entrepreneurs, one an aviation pioneer and the other an industrialist. I was fortunate to be able to spend a lot of time with both of them as I was growing up, and they were both important role models.

My uncle, George "Arky" Vaughn, is an entrepreneur, and I recall the day when I was a little kid he was over at our cottage in Lake Placid one evening for cocktails and he announced he was leaving his steady job at an aluminum company to create a start-up focused on aluminum fabrications. I think my parents thought he was crazy to leave a solid, well-paying job, but Arky loved to play tennis and he saw the potential of using aluminum to create a better tennis racket, among other things. My grandparents dipped into their savings to provide some initial capital. I remember quite vividly when Arky excitedly took my brother and me to the top floor of a big red potato barn in the countryside near Princeton, NJ, to show us his "operation," which consisted of a couple of hand-operated machines he had designed to shape the aluminum into tennis racquet frames. And there was my Aunt Martha at the end of the line as "quality control" and putting stickers on the bases of the rackets. The company was originally called Maark, which was derived from the first letters of their respective names, "ma" for Martha and "ark" for Arky. It was my first exposure to a start-up. Arky eventually reached a marketing deal with Head Corporation, and his Head Master tennis racquet became a huge hit and changed the game of tennis. He also manufactured the first oversized racquet called the Prince, which was an even "bigger" game changer. I'm grateful that Arky took the time that day to show us his start-up, well before it took off.

Aside from family, I have to acknowledge all my close friends that also put up with my crazy ideas and what I am sure sound like random ramblings. I often call on them for advice, and they are always there with help. They know who they are, and I love them dearly!

I am blessed indeed to be working with each and every one of my colleagues at LoveToKnow. It is an incredible team and it is a privilege, as well as a ton of fun, to be working with them.

I have to acknowledge all of the wonderful entrepreneurs I have had the pleasure of working with. It's with them that I have learned the lessons contained in this book, and we learned them together. I'll try to list a few: Byron Reese, Sara Fell, Sam Shank, Cliff Ribaudo, Peter Handsman, Jim Williams, Jeff Rayfield, Clem Bason, Jonathan Rickert, Doug Colbeck, Sean Muller, Hein Van Wyk, Feagal Mac Conuladh, Mark Box, Evan Reece, Gordon Schaeffer, Anne Nichols, Lance Black, Pete Flint, and Sami Inkinen.

David and I are lucky to have fantastic lawyers that we work with: David Marks, Buddy Arnheim, and DJ Drennan. They've helped David and me on many deals and kept us out of trouble, which we are quite grateful for. They are also all great guys that are fun to work with.

I had a talented writer, Bruce Wexler, help me write this book, and there is no doubt that this is a way better book because of his help and guidance. His experience, his insightful questions, and his steady pace made this book happen.

There are some wonderful writings on entrepreneurship that I think are exceptional and highly recommend:

- Paul Graham—His essays are published online, and anyone who aspires to be an entrepreneur needs to read these.

- Sam Altman—His Playbook essay is one of the single best essays available. Sam works with Paul Graham, so you will see similarities.

- Marc Andreesen—Essay on product/market fit. It's a single essay, and though I don't agree with it entirely, I agree with it mostly, and it's one that you should read.

- Geoffrey Moore—*Crossing the Chasm*. This is one of the original books on start-ups and I've read it a number of times. Geoff's bowling pin analogy is still one I refer to regularly when discussing how to enter a market.

- Eric Ries—*Lean Startup*. This book is incredibly helpful, especially in the Morph phase of your start-up, a must-read.

- Ben Horowitz—*The Hard Thing About Hard Things*.

- Peter Thiel—*Zero to One*, a great book from a guy with an incredible track record. Highly recommend reading, especially his views on competition.

- Tarang Shah—*Venture Capitalists at Work*

- Jessica Livingston—*Founders at Work*

- Richard Branson—I've read all of Sir Richard's books and they are great, with lots of helpful advice as well as the key mantra—have fun!

Finally, I want to acknowledge my publisher, Greenleaf Book Group, that has been so helpful and professional. They have guided me every step of the way with helpful advice, direction, and work. The entire team has been supportive of this project from the time I met them, and I am grateful!

ABOUT THE AUTHOR

Howard Love has been starting companies for more than thirty years, even prior to his graduation from Colgate University in 1983. He has founded or co-founded over fifteen companies and invested in over fifty early stage start-ups. He has led several of these companies himself as well as advising many others. He has served on numerous public and private company boards and is currently on the boards of directors of FlexJobs, Dealbase, Hotel-Tonight, 10 Foot Wave, and Knowingly. Mr. Love also owns and operates LoveToKnow, a digital media publisher that he started in 2004. LoveToKnow's primary media properties are LoveToKnow.com, YourDictionary.com, and GolfLink.com. He has lived in Silicon Valley for the past twenty-five years with his wife, Harriet, and three children. For more information, visit howardlove.com.